Barns
Styles & Structures

Michael Karl Witzel

MBI

This edition first published in 2003 by Motorbooks International, an imprint of MBI Publishing Company, Galtier Plaza, Suite 200, 380 Jackson Street, St. Paul, MN 55101-3885 USA

Dedication

Barns: Styles and Structures
is dedicated to that
overall-wearing,
seed-planting,
tractor-driving,
down-to-earth individual
known as the American farmer
and to the vanishing institution
known as
the family farm.

The information in this book is true and complete to the best of our knowledge. All recommendations are made without any guarantee on the part of the author or Publisher, who also disclaim any liability incurred in connection with the use of this data or specific details.

We recognize that some words, model names and designations, for example, mentioned herein are the property of the trademark holder. We use them for identification purposes only. This is not an official publication.

Motorbooks International titles are also available at discounts in bulk quantity for industrial or sales-promotional use. For details write to Special Sales Manager at Motorbooks International Wholesalers & Distributors, Galtier Plaza, Suite 200, 380 Jackson Street, St. Paul, MN 55101-3885 USA.

ISBN 0-7603-1608-2

Editor: Amy Glaser
Designer: LeAnn Kuhlmann
Printed in China

On the front cover: This quiet scene in Waterman, Illinois, speaks of a new day and the rewards of the hard work that lies ahead. *©2003 Howard Ande, Coolstock.com*

On the frontispiece: The interior framework of the Angola, Indiana, round barn demonstrates just how sound circular construction methods could be. *©2003 Keith Baum, Coolstock.com*

On the title page: Sunrise in Brownstown, Pennsylvania, reveals multiple rooftop ventilators and a grain silo. *©2003 Keith Baum, Coolstock.com*

On the contents page: The exterior siding of this saltbox style barn in Kaneville, Illinois, is evidence of an architectural evolution. *©2003 Howard Ande, Coolstock.com*

On the back cover: The repeating sheaves of wheat pattern incorporated into this brick-end bank barn in Lititz, Pennsylvania, was added to provide a practical means of ventilating the stored hay. *©2003 Keith Baum, Coolstock.com*

Today, operations like this Archbold, Ohio, farm concentrate on raising livestock, an endeavor augmented by the capabilities of the modern silo. *©2003 Keith Baum, Coolstock.com*

At the end: The gambrel roof was a boon to farmers when it was first introduced. With the added space, enough food could be stored to feed the animals through the winter months. *©2003 Keith Baum, Coolstock.com*

Contents

Preface

My childhood memories are filled with long, leisurely drives through the scenic countryside of New Jersey. Visions of green fields, grazing cows, roaming sheep, statuesque grain silos, towering trees, white wooden fences, and stately barns dominate my recollections.

To some, New Jersey might seem an unlikely place to cultivate an appreciation for barns and the unique variations of utilitarian American architecture. Routinely portrayed in the media as an urban annex to New York City and used as the frequent butt of jokes, this New England state is much maligned.

Let's face it: When it comes to scenic beauty, people who hail from regions outside of the tri-state area of New York, New Jersey, and Connecticut often imagine this land to be comprised of only chemical dumps, butcher shops, nuclear waste sites, and run-down tenements. For many, it's the epitome of the asphalt jungle.

This interpretation of New Jersey couldn't be farther from the truth. Sure, there are urban areas that lack any sort of beauty, but no more than in any other state. In reality, the Garden State boasts a landscape rich with fertile fields, vigorous farm animals, and bucolic farm sights. Here are the statistics: In the year 2000, the U.S. Department of Agriculture reported that there were some 9,600 farms in the state that used 830,000 acres of land. On those farms are countless structures designed for agricultural uses, including barns.

This is the scenery that I remember from the weekend jaunts in the family car, far from the hustle and bustle of the turnpike, toll-roads, and the roar of traffic. In my mind's eye, I can still see the greenery rushing past as my father piloted the car over hill and dale, bringing us always closer to the new visual experiences that waited for us around the bend.

Sure, I'm from Jersey. Classic barns are from there, too.

—Michael Karl Witzel
    Austin, Texas
    May 2003

Opposite: Maybe life on the farm isn't changing after all. A 1935 John Deere Model B Brass Tag Edition and a classic red barn, both owned by Allen Martin of Ephrata, Pennsylvania, remind us of the way farming used to be. ©2003 Keith Baum, Coolstock.com

Chapter One

Dutch Barn

By Divine Influence

Before Jamestown, Virginia, was established, nothing in North America stood taller than the native forests and grasses. That changed in 1620. The Dutch settlers who plowed the indigenous sod also dotted the virgin landscapes with towering, stately structures, creations that had never before been seen on the continent. Barns—functional buildings designed to enable a self-sustaining lifestyle—popped up like so many cornstalks to provide immigrant farmers with reliable shelter and a base of operations to conduct their livelihoods.

This initial building boom of barns began in a resource-rich region of New England within the boundaries known today as New York state. Here, under the direction of the Dutch West India Company, immigrants arrived hoping to establish a foothold in the New World. At the mouth of the Hudson River, the Dutch established the settlement called New Netherland, an outpost reminiscent of the old country, strong in trade and shipping.

Keen to master this new domain, wealthy Dutch landowners, or patroons, established large estates in the Hudson, Mohawk, and Schoharie valleys. The Dutch also settled along New Jersey's Hackensack, Passaic, Raritan, and Millstone rivers and their tributaries. In exchange for prime waterfront real estate, the well-to-do patrons pledged to sponsor 50 new settlers and bring them over from Holland within four years.

As the dinner bell rings and the farm equipment is stowed for the night, another day on the farm ends in Union Grove, Illinois. ©2003 Howard Ande, Coolstock.com

Whether the participants are Mennonite, Amish, Shaker, or members of any other denomination, barn raising is perhaps the quintessential example of neighbor helping neighbor. It is an activity that is witnessed frequently in the farming community. ©2003 Keith Baum, Coolstock.com

The patroon was much like the feudal lord of the Middle Ages. As a benevolent master, it was his responsibility to provide his tenants with a house, a parcel of land, and sometimes a small barn. He was also expected to provide a minister and a schoolteacher and to stock his tenants' farms with tools and cattle. In effect, he owned the tenants who were under his tutelage.

To uphold their part of the bargain, tenants paid rent and maintained a fixed place of living for 10 years. Farming was the de facto occupation, and residents were required to use the patroon's mill to grind their corn. Weaving fabric wasn't allowed, and textiles had to be purchased from the storehouse. Hunting and fishing also required permission.

While it was an opportunity for tenants to begin a new life in the colonies, the patroon system didn't get much admiration from the English. In fact, the growing settlements posed a threat to England's long-range plans. The ever-widening Dutch expansion was viewed as an obstacle to England's own growth. To quell the insurgence,

This Plato Center, Illinois, barn is ready for the cold winter months. Keeping the weather out of the barn has always been a difficult task, but modern materials and construction methods have made interior temperature control much easier. ©2003 Howard Ande, Coolstock.com

King Charles II sent a fleet of ships to attack the colony at New Amsterdam and recover what he believed was rightfully his.

In 1664, New Netherland fell to the English without a fight. Ironically, the Dutch settlers welcomed English rule. Their allegiance was weakened by a disdain for their sponsor's restrictions and their lack of representation in the government. This show of displaced loyalty was inconsequential to the king's brother, the Duke of York. He assumed ownership of the newly conquered territory and promptly renamed the burgeoning melting pot "New York."

Although they no longer held political control, the Dutch continued to exert influence on the New York region, most notably in the realm of vernacular architecture. Fifty years of unfettered reign gave them ample time to leave a distinctive signature on the native modes of construction. During this span, the builders of countless farmsteads redefined the concepts of form, function, and execution that had been passed down to them from their ancestors. In the end, the architecture of the Dutch

As shown on this 1906 Crosley Brothers' barn in Kansas, the gable entry used in early examples of the Dutch barn has influenced countless iterations of the American farm structure. ©2003 Dan Harlow, Coolstock.com

barn emerged as a symbol of their cultural influence—integral to the *lingua franca* of rural New England architecture.

The characteristic elements that define the genus "Dutch barn" take us all the way back to iron-age Britain. When it came time to build a practical structure designed to support farming during the fourth century B.C., necessity was surely proven to be the mother of invention. The time-honored practice of using the most convenient materials on hand ruled the day, and wood, earth, and stone topped the list of barn-building materials.

The first barn prototypes were rectangular, braced at each end with timbers hand-crafted from oak, sweet chestnut, or black poplar trees. Medieval carpenters sought out sturdy trunks that exhibited a natural bend, which allowed them to split the wood apart at the center in order to create two identical blades. Once they were stripped of their branches, these timbers were planted upright and embedded in walls of chalk or sarsen stone about one meter from ground level.

At the apex of these bent beams, wooden pegs or a collar beam tied the two pieces together to form a curved "A." A secondary tie beam positioned a few feet below provided additional support for the purlins needed to support the rafters. Formed with nature's assistance, this unique style of supporting brace was known as a cruck and was the basis for the entire structure.

To tie the skeleton together, builders attached a ridgepole between the crucks. The curved walls were equally simple in composition. They were formed using a technique known as "wattle and daub." To strengthen the assembly, the spaces between the crucks and ridgepole were interwoven with a tight network of wooden staves, branches, or twigs. In later variations of cruck homes and barns, a more conventional, rectangular frame was combined with the curved supports to provide the option for straight, angular walls.

For the daub, the rigid framework was filled with any number of ready-made materials, including a rather odoriferous mixture of cattle manure and straw. In later

centuries, builders used an infilling of brick and mortar. After this early form of quick-set concrete was worked into place by hand, the walls were finished off with a smooth application of homemade stucco. Fortified with horse hair, this mixture of lime-plaster provided a bright, finished look.

The wooden lattice-work of the frame remained exposed to the exterior and created the dramatic contrast of whitewash and wood that was typical of early cruck-style architecture. The roof was a point of visual interest as well, hipped by nature and described by Eric Arthur and Dudley Whitney in *The Barn: A Vanishing Landmark in North America* as "unforgettable, powerful, proof against all weathers, and marvelously manicured in reed thatch."

When viewed on end, the homes and barns erected with the cruck method of framing recalled the distinctive shape of a ship's hull, albeit an upturned one. This unique design archetype was also found in the great Christian cathedrals of the age. The curved blades of the crucks in the barns of the Old World replicated the dramatic vaulting found in the Gothic halls of worship. Inside the Dutch barn, a long central hall was flanked by an aisle on each side, and copied the configuration of the typical church nave (the word *nave* originates from the Latin *navis*, or *ship*). Massive wood timbers were substituted for polished stone columns. The space that typically held the congregation was used to house farm animals. Because of these interior characteristics, historians refer to the Dutch design as basilican.

After it was exported to the colonies and the settlement called New Netherland, the basilican arrangement became a showcase for the masterful carpentry of the Dutch builders. Inside, many of the standard barn construction techniques were

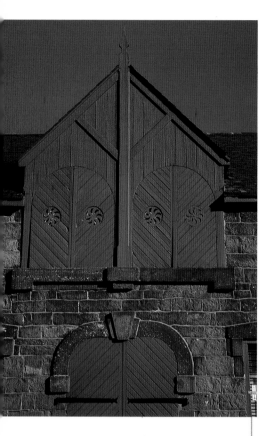

Germanic design elements, executed in bold stone relief and the artful arrangement of wood planks, characterize this horse-barn dormer detail in Cornwall Furnace, Pennsylvania. ©2003 Keith Baum, Coolstock.com

This weathered northern California example is reminiscent of the low-eave Dutch designs that were first seen in Europe. Doors located to each side of the main entry provided access to the bays that housed animals. ©2003 Keith Baum, Coolstock.com

followed. Mortised, tenoned, and pegged beams were arranged in H-shaped supports. Wall girts were used to strengthen the structure. Sapling poles comprised the loft floor. Chamfered diagonal braces provided additional support where beams married posts. Rafters and purlins supported the roof.

There was also a new twist added to the standard techniques of joinery. To distinguish the massive cross-beams that were supported by the central columns, Dutch carpenters finished the ends with flat, rounded tongues. These projections fit through a mating slot in the adjoining support and were secured using hardwood pegs, or treenails. Without precedence, this carpentry technique became a distinctive signature of Dutch barn architecture. Today it exists as an identifier that is unique to the genre.

While the tongue-end beam treatment was visually pleasing, decoration wasn't the goal of the New World barn builders. Space for work and storage was the primary concern, and the sturdy framework provided abundant interior room. The center aisle of the Dutch barn is spacious to allow the farmer to load and unload wagons and take care of the threshing activities. Typically the work area inside spans a distance

that is equal to three (and up to five) of the horizontal H-frame anchor beams. This space is repeated in the loft above where sapling poles support sheaves of stored hay.

The side aisles flank the 20- to 30-foot section. These occupy the remainder of the barn's interior and are divided up to house a full complement of creatures. Near the gable end at the front, the standard practice was to house pigs in a small pen on one side and calves in their own pen on the opposite side. The remaining area ran the length of the walls and was divided into multiple stalls to hold livestock. Cattle were penned on one side, and horses were stabled on the other. It was a time-saving setup for the farmer since the stanchioned animals faced inward and could be readily fed and watered from the central nave.

This arrangement stemmed from the original plan followed in Holland and greater Europe, where the family, servants, and animals lived in the same structure. According to M. E. Christie, author of *Evolution of the English Farm*, the home-cum-barn hybrid was a style of farmstead that dominated the continent since time immemorial and was "common to all Aryan peoples at an early stage of their development." The Saxon house incorporated all of the aspects of the barn, byre, and house under one contiguous roof.

In the earliest examples of these multipurpose dwellings, the living area was simply an extension of the threshing floor. Later, a common household space divided the living quarters from the rest of the barn and individual rooms separated family activities from farming activities. At the residence end of the threshing floor, a large hearth held a peat fire that smoldered around the clock. Because the barn housed so much combustible material (such as wood timbers, hay, and feed), open fires or

This barn, located in northern California, illustrates how the influence of barn builders spread from coast to coast. ©2003 Sylvester Allred, Coolstock.com

The Pennsylvania Dutch are well known for their colorful hex signs that are prominently displayed on countless barns in the region. Whether they are intended to attract good luck or ward off evil, they add a distinctive signature that is remembered by locals and tourists alike. ©2003 Keith Baum, Coolstock.com

Sporting a raised, monitor-like roof projection, this Wasco, Illinois, barn is a survivor. Many of the substantial barns built during the 1800s endure to this day, which is a testament to the ingenuity and craftsmanship of their builders. ©2003 Bruce Leighty, Coolstock.com

lamps were shunned. The old English proverb "a lantern on the table is death in the stable" was not hyperbole.

Different types of rooms, all with different purposes, were found at this end of the barn. They included a storeroom, living room, and best room. Workers and servants slept one level above the animals. The women's quarters were located on one side of the loft, while manservants held court on the other side of the gallery.

This practice of combining home and barn quickly changed after the Dutch set up their respective farming operations in North America. Immigrants didn't live under the same roof as their animals. Historical accounts cite that early settlers had to be self-sufficient and provide the majority of their necessities themselves, so most efforts were focused on producing a crop, not on homebuilding.

The stereotypical image of a weathered gray barn, stocked with tractors and other farming equipment, holds a special place in the hearts and minds of Americans raised in both small towns and big cities. ©2003 Keith Baum, Coolstock.com

It often took farmers several years of hard work before they could clear and plant a sufficient amount of land to produce a surplus. When this level was achieved, the money earned from the sale of the excess allowed for the purchase or trade of durable goods. In the meantime, a simple roofed dugout or a log cabin provided adequate shelter.

Because the family no longer occupied space at one end of the barn, subtle modifications to the basilican design were possible. The first update was to modify the tradition of the single large entrance. By the time the patroon system was extinct, the Dutch barns that were built in New York state featured double wagon doors on each end to allow wagons to pass directly through the structure without backing up. This end drive design greatly augmented the utility of the barn. It complemented the winnowing process since the diametrically positioned openings provided the draft necessary for the time-honored chore of separating kernel from husk and wheat from chaff.

With all of the new openings being punched into the walls of the Dutch barn, special considerations were made for the door design. To that end, Dutch carpenters contributed to the functional evolution of the barn when they popularized the

Rooftop cupolas provide a necessary function for all types of barns. Ventilation is their primary purpose, but barn owners also find them useful for mounting weather vanes, lightning rods, and other decorative elements. ©2003 Keith Baum, Coolstock.com

Kutztown, Pennsylvania, is home to the Pinnacle Winery. This structure is a prominent example of a barn remodeled for uses other than agriculture. It showcases how thoughtful design and quality construction can transcend the ages and its intended purpose. ©2003 Ron Saari, Coolstock.com

so-called Dutch door, a portal divided into two horizontal halves and hinged so that one or the other may be opened or closed independently.

Unlike the esoteric cross-beam tongues that characterized the interior supports, Dutch doors became *de rigueur* for practical barns. In fact, their use was so widespread that books detailed the standards for construction. In the 1913 edition of *Modern Farm Buildings*, Alfred Hopkins specified, "The lower half of a Dutch door should be 4 feet, 6 inches high for horses, and for cattle, 3 feet, 8 inches is high enough. All Dutch doors should open out and be arranged to hook back flat against the building." Over time, Dutch barn architecture had proven itself, and it carried its influence well into the twentieth century.

Wood was the primary material used to construct the doors as well as almost every other part of the New World Dutch barn. With the widespread availability of timber, the use of wattle and daub was outmoded. Extra-wide clapboards graced the exterior and were nailed horizontally over the frame studs. Atop the broad and steep gabled roofs, cedar shingles rendered thatch a vestige of old and provided a durable alternative to resist rain. The threshing floor also received a makeover. Instead of featuring the hard-packed earth used in the early prototypes, the improved barn featured a deck lined with heavy wooden planks.

With its Dutch doors, solid structure, end-drive access, broad gabled roof, ample space for livestock, oversized space for threshing, and basilican design, the New World Dutch barn was built in great numbers. Between 1620 and 1835, the new design changed the face of the rural landscape in North America and forged a path for centuries of American barn builders to follow. It arrived in the New World as a hybrid and quickly evolved into a structure of distinction. In the centuries to come, the New World Dutch barn endured as a monument to craftsmanship, ingenuity, and hard work. It was a potent example of what humans could achieve with a little divine inspiration.

With its low roofline and gable entry, this Dutch-inspired structure mates with a larger gambrel-roofed example to present a connected configuration that melds a variety of architectural styles and influences. ©2003 Bruce Leighty, Coolstock.com

Like the house and barn combinations integrated under one roof in old Europe, this Platte City, Missouri, barn shows how a well-tried concept can be adapted for modern use. It houses a variety of facilities under a series of connected roofs and is a structure ready to meet the variety of demands placed upon it. ©2003 Ron Saari, Coolstock.com

Its red paint is weathered and faded, but this decaying barn in Cool Springs, Tennessee, speaks of fruitful harvests and a well-used life. ©2003 Howard Ande, Coolstock.com

A stovepipe installed in the roof of this Ridgeway, Colorado, barn is evidence that this structure may also be used for owner accommodations or to house the farm hands. ©2003 Howard Ande, Coolstock.com

This Amish dairy barn in Gordonville, Pennsylvania, proves the more things change, the more they stay the same. The Amish still use a horse and buggy, equipped with reflectors for safety and traffic regulations, for transport. ©2003 Keith Baum, Coolstock.com

An ample hayloft is required to feed cattle and other animals throughout the winter season. This stout cattle barn is located in Montana. ©2003 Sylvester Allred, Coolstock.com

Historically, barns have been painted red, green, and black. Bright blue was the unconventional color choice for the owner of this striking Darlington, Maryland, gambrel-roof barn. ©2003 Keith Baum, Coolstock.com

23

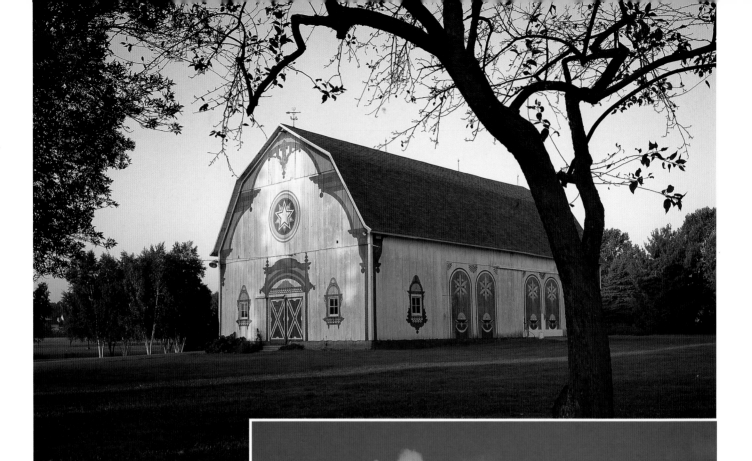

In the early development of the barn, ornamentation was discouraged and deemed unessential for the basic function of the structure. Today decorative embellishments, like those gracing this Pennsylvania barn, showcase the humor and imagination of their owners. ©2003 Keith Baum, Coolstock.com

This gambrel-roof barn near Pomeroy, Ohio, has evidence of heavy use. This end drive design was a configuration that served farmers for centuries and allowed equipment to be driven directly in and out the other side. ©2003 Keith Baum, Coolstock.com

Painted in all colors of the rainbow, decorative wall murals are a common sight along the rural highways and byways of America. The broad side of a barn is the perfect canvas for all manner of decoration, including portraits of prominent farm animals. ©2003 Keith Baum, Coolstock.com

In small, rural farming towns like Quarryville, Pennsylvania, decorative lights grace many barns to ring in the good cheer of the holiday season. The farming community revolves around people and always seems friendly and welcoming. ©2003 Keith Baum, Coolstock.com

This red-and-white barn combines the stone foundation of its numerous barn predecessors with a gambrel roof, and it conjures up memories of playing in the haymow and helping with the chores.
©2003 Keith Baum, Coolstock.com

Rather than subscribe to a style of construction derived from a single architectural lineage, modern barns take inspiration from many sources. This Hunterdon County, New Jersey, barn is an amalgam of barn-building history, complete with a large haymow, natural stone foundation, cross-X door treatments, and grain silo. ©2003 Ron Saari, Coolstock.com

Chapter Two

Pennsylvania Barn

Functional Forebay

Before the first shot was fired in the Revolutionary War, the English restricted immigration to the North American colonies and barred nationalities deemed unhelpful to their cause. During this time, most of the new settlers who arrived in America were German or German-speaking Swiss. They imported a heritage steeped in architectural ingenuity. These immigrants clustered in the regions of southeastern Pennsylvania and established homes and farmsteads throughout the counties of Northampton, Berks, Lancaster, Lehigh, Montgomery, and Bucks.

The Pennsylvania Dutch (as they were called) conceived, planned, and constructed many of the finest barns in North America. One timber at a time, they raised the bar of vernacular architecture and handily surpassed many of the best Dutch and English examples. With an eye toward ergonomics, amenability to livestock, and adaptation to local conditions, they enhanced the North American landscape with beautiful, practical structures. Today these exemplary specimens are classified as Pennsylvania-German barns.

That's were the butter churn tips over. Contrary to popular belief, the people known as the Pennsylvania Dutch aren't Dutch descendants, but are instead of German and German-speaking heritage. The Oxford English Dictionary describes the Pennsylvania Dutch as "descendants of the original German settlers in Pennsylvania."

A mix of German, Dutch, English, and other influences, this red-and-white charmer near Lebanon, Pennsylvania, is designed for maximum efficiency. The animals are located below, the haymow is above, and the adjoining sheds store tools and equipment. ©2003 Keith Baum, Coolstock.com

By all accounts, it seems that this cultural identity crisis got its start during the fifteenth and sixteenth centuries when the English labeled all people of Germanic heritage as Dutch. It didn't help matters that the German word for *German* is *Deutsch*. Speaking with a heavy accent, a farmer who introduced himself as a "Deutschman" didn't convey the fact he was German. English speakers thought they heard "Dutchman" and falsely assumed that the individual was from Holland.

This point is key since these memorable Pennsylvania barns have no connection with the Netherlands. According to T. J. Wertenbaker, the author of *The Founding of American Civilization: The Middle Colonies*, the ancestry of the Pennsylvania-German barn is actually rooted within the "wooded highlands of Upper Bavaria, the southern spur of the Black Mountains, and in the Jura region and elsewhere in Switzerland."

The barn at the Daniel Boone Homestead incorporates many of the design elements found in the typical Pennsylvania-German barns, with the addition of a side shed. ©2003 Keith Baum, Coolstock.com

In this Germanic region of stately mountains and deep valleys, there was little flat land to build upon. Farmers carved out a homestead from the hillsides, and they modified farm and domestic structures to work in harmony with the lay of the land. The builders of homes and barns leveraged the features of the surrounding terrain and took advantage of the indigenous slopes. By positioning a barn lengthwise, at a right angle to a hill, a farmer could gain easy access to the second story without the use of an additional ramp.

On the top level, the all-important haymow and threshing floor occupied the bulk of available square footage. Meanwhile, the family took residence in a smaller, adjacent compartment positioned directly at the front of the structure. Here a prow-shaped roof extension granted protection from the high mountain winds. To keep the roof on, residents weighed it down with stones. Shuttered windows kept out the harsh weather and gave the family a view of the animals grazing in the valley below. A surrounding porch with a fenced railing provided additional *lebensraum* (or living space) outside.

One story below, where the cattle, sheep, and pigs were penned, a stone foundation cradled the overhanging wood frame and kept out the cold and frost. Here wood timbers of various gauge were used for the floor joists, vertical structural supports, and remainder of the upper framing. Taking stock of the various farm, family, and livestock compartments contained therein, the narrow, rectangular footprint of this structure stretched out to 100 feet or more.

To add extra space on the second floor, builders projected the top story floor joists outward and copied the centuries-old style of military architecture that relied on the extended, overhanging frame bay that was employed for various defensive reasons. This feature emerged as the single-most memorable design element of the style and directly influenced the German and Swiss barns that were soon to be built in North America.

When the Swiss Mennonites fled to the English colonies to escape persecution, they brought the best of this hybrid design with them and continued to combine

Stone, in its many shapes and forms, has been incorporated in the design of barns since their inception. Thanks to the work of a skilled mason, a stone wall or foundation can last for centuries. ©2003 Ron Saari, Coolstock.com

In Carol County, Maryland, it's not unusual to encounter grand interpretations of the overhanging bank barn, complete with decorative ventilation louvers and a trio of rooftop cupolas. ©2003 Keith Baum, Coolstock.com

Barns adorned with hex signs are common sights along Route 73 in Shanesville, Pennsylvania. ©2003 Ron Saari, Coolstock.com

living quarters for the family, agricultural facilities for processing crops, and a byre for animals into one structure. There was one conspicuous distinction that set their barns apart from those of their European forebears: The settlers of southern Pennsylvania built their barns parallel to the hill. In both the German Palatinate region and the Canton Bern of Switzerland, the barns were built at right angles to the lie of the hill.

Due in large part to this new orientation, the natural architectural progression was to add a cantilevered overhang that spanned the entire front of the structure. The family quarters were removed and replaced by extra threshing compartments, a granary, and a place to store sheaves of wheat.

If the surrounding land allowed this extended portion to face south, it was pure serendipity for the farmer. In this instance, farm animals could be sheltered from the northerly winds while they remained outdoors in a protected, open-air byre. Known as a "laube," this sheltered porch, or overhang, became a defining element of Pennsylvania-German folk architecture.

If one hex sign is said to bring good luck, why not try three? The Pennsylvania-Dutch region is famous for these graphic symbols. Every year tourists snap up an endless supply of reproductions. ©*2003 Keith Baum, Coolstock.com*

The gargantuan timbers available to the builders and carpenters of the day were integral to the execution of this striking, cantilevered design. Massive trunks felled in well-stocked, virgin forests provided the overarching support required to distribute the load of the upper extension. Adzed beams stretched from the upper doorsill at the back to the livestock wall and beyond. These large beams were set on 3-foot centers and straddled the structure's width to provide unencumbered space beneath the forebay. In some cases, the beams were 50 feet long, and length of the mow overhang measured as much as 8 feet.

Like the prototypes built in Europe, these early Pennsylvania barns were planned in coordination with a nearby hillside to allow simple ground-level access to both floors. When there was no naturally occurring rise for barn builders to take

In Lancaster, Pennsylvania, this rock and wood bank barn, complete with extended laube, houses livestock on the lower level. Multiple doors allow access to various bays, and the cantilevered extension provides enhanced protection from the weather. ©2003 Keith Baum, Coolstock.com

advantage of, an artificial bank was formed by building an earthen ramp up to the mow floor on the second level.

On the lowest level, the protection given from the adjoining hillside made for an excellent frost-free space to store root crops such as turnips. In some of the larger bank barns, there was also enough space in the basement to house a half dozen horses on one side, a row of milking cows on the other, and three more bays of cows and calves in the center. The Pennsylvania-German barn was designed for serious farming and livestock management and had room leftover for a couple of feed mangers as well as an area for feed bins and root choppers.

With this new conjugation of styles, the seeds of ingenuity grew and blossomed to give credence to a new style of farm-friendly barn. Its practical features were numerous. Its lengthwise hill orientation offered quick and easy access to multiple threshing bays on the second story, and trap doors in the floor allowed fodder to be dropped to the animals below to streamline the chore of feeding. Barns of this ilk were built with as many as three threshing bays to provide the farmer with the work space demanded by large-scale farming. Extra space to store the winnowed grain and sheaves of wheat awaiting threshing tied it all together.

Inside, the Pennsylvania barn was much like the other basilican-style barns erected during the same period. The mow was divided into aisles or galleries with a central space, or nave. Massive posts divided this space, adzed into shape by the carpenters of old, as were the beams, purlins, rafters, and other major structural members. The components of the internal framework were precut and numbered to fit together with mortise and tenons. Because of the Pennsylvania-German barn builders' aversion to technology, nails weren't used. Oak pegs were the only acceptable method to lock the pieces of pine together.

As axes chopped and buzz saws ripped, wood was pressed into service for almost everything imaginable. Eventually this widespread use of wooden pegs, support beams, posts, roofing shingles, flooring, and siding affected the size and type of lumber available. By the 1830s, the spiraling demands brought about by the Northeast's hunger for wood products put supplies in jeopardy. "Well may ours be called a wooden country," declared James Hall, "not merely from the extent of its forests, but because in common use, wood has been substituted for a number of most necessary . . . articles such as stone, iron, and even leather."

The Mennonite barn raising is a ritual that is still practiced with regular frequency. When a barn burns down or is destroyed by another disaster, neighbors band together to erect a new structure. For the members of this faith, it's an insurance policy based on a trust in people. ©2003 Keith Baum, Coolstock.com

Gable-end ventilation holes arranged in a variety of whimsical patterns are a striking characteristic of many classic Pennsylvania-German barns. ©2003 Keith Baum, Coolstock.com

To make matters worse, the iron furnaces that dotted the countryside were voracious consumers of firewood. A single day of operation could burn up as much as 360 bushels of charcoal. Typical for operations of the era, the Union Furnace in New Jersey was responsible for 20,000 acres of forest going up in smoke in less than 15 years. Because wood was in such high demand for homes, barns, durable goods, and even common household fuel used in inefficient home fireplaces, much of the North American coastal plain was denuded of trees by the early nineteenth century.

Forests were no longer able to replenish the stands of immense trees that were used to form massive swing beams and other structural supports. The techniques used today to join smaller pieces of wood together to form a strong laminate were centuries away. So, rather than discontinue the structurally sound overshoot typical of the large bank barn, builders supported the overhanging laube with more conventional pillars and posts. Stone or concrete columns set at spaced intervals provided stable footings to hold the structure in place.

In some instances, Pennsylvania barn designs were built without the forebay and precluded the need for the normally stout support setup. Here the livestock wall and the lower portion of the mow were aligned in the same vertical plane. To protect the windows and doors below from roof run-off, a pentice, or lean-to roof projection ratio of 2-to-3, was added. The same style of deflector was often seen on the upper level directly over the wagon doors.

As the forebay style of barn evolved, brick became a popular building material and was used in many of the finest examples of Pennsylvania-German barns. In some of the earliest examples, the narrow-end side walls were frequently constructed of interlocking courses and followed the setup technique of English bond (every sixth course of bricks is a row of headers) and Flemish bond (header bricks follow the stretchers in every course). Walls of this type were as much as 16 inches thick and were impervious to failure and virtually unaffected by time.

Here the configuration of stone and mortar was far from conventional. Creative brick masons used the gable ends of the barns as canvases for whimsical patterns and purposely omitted stones to form a variety of striking pictograms similar to the blocky pixels of a modern computer graphic. In striking contrast to the Amish and Mennonite practice of shunning ornamentation, the customs of these barn builders allowed for creative ventilation patterns. Patterns included an "X", a square grid, a triangle, an unfolding lily, a wine goblet, a vertical slot, a bushel measure, and even an evergreen tree. Perhaps the undeniable functionality of these vents allowed them to slip through the restrictions of the Ordnung, the Amish rules of living.

Regardless of religious doctrine, the clever groupings of wall holes managed to transcend their intended purpose of increasing airflow through the barn to inhibit the spontaneous combustion of curing hay. When viewed from the inside, the rising or setting sun energized the patterns with an almost ethereal, luminous glow. The effect was awe-inspiring, if not magical.

Massive Pennsylvania-German barns still survive in the regions in and around Boyertown, Pennsylvania. This multistoried behemoth incorporates wine glass–shaped ventilation holes in the gables and sash windows all around.
©2003 Keith Baum, Coolstock.com

The bank barn isn't always constructed on a drastic incline. The effect is often subtle and has just enough of a rise to allow access to the second level.
©2003 Keith Baum, Coolstock.com

The magic of this type of barn wasn't restricted to the eye-pleasing arrangement of the brick ventilation holes that beautified some of the classic examples. The Pennsylvania Dutch barn was also known for its use of exterior adornment, most particularly the colorful, circular hex signs that were painted or hung on exteriors throughout the region.

Hex signs featured a series of geometric patterns or symmetrical designs filled with primary colors and were painted directly onto the surface of the barn. Later they were painted onto wooden discs and attached with nails or screws.

The original purpose of these hex signs is still debated today, although many folklorists agree that various cultures throughout the ages have associated graphic patterns with magical symbolism. According to some historical accounts, the hexafoos, or witchfoot as they are sometimes called, were first brought over from the Rhineland in Germany during the seventeenth century. In the German dialect spoken by the Pennsylvania Dutch, *hexe* was the equivalent of the German verb

Bank barns can be found all across the country, as shown by this red-and-white example in Leelanau, Michigan. Double weather vanes, rooftop flags, and a colorful paint job display patriotism. ©2003 Keith Baum, Coolstock.com

Grand bank barns, such as this Lenhartsville, Pennsylvania, model, are at the heart of many farming operations in the region. Here an extended wall was constructed around the perimeter of the byre to create a pen. ©2003 Keith Baum, Coolstock.com

hexen, which meant "to practice sorcery." When they first settled in the colonies, the Amish and Mennonites employed them as a type of demoniac lightning rod in hopes of warding off cow-fever and other evil influences, including curses levied by neighbors.

Despite these accounts, many of the Pennsylvania old-timers insist that the colorful hex signs were used only for decoration. As they say in the local parlance, hex signs were painted "chust for nice." But if one takes into account the religious beliefs of many of the sectarian groups that dominated the area, it would seem rather illogical to believe that hex signs and symbols were created for no real purpose but ornamentation. It makes more sense to suppose that hex patterns were a kind of painted prayer—a good luck charm used to ensure the fertility of livestock, invoke success of crops, or summon favorable weather.

Today this spirit of decoration still thrives in the farming regions of southern Pennsylvania and beyond. From the roadside, admiring travelers may still spy a multitude of graphic patterns and murals that adorn the outer walls of barns and

With two sliding haymow doors, this Nazareth, Pennsylvania, bank barn combines the storage efficiency of the gambrel roof with the practicality of integrated overshoot supported by columns. ©*2003 Keith Baum, Coolstock.com*

41

The stone-end barn at historic Rock Ford in Lancaster, Pennsylvania, showcases the typical placement of the bank barn and takes advantage of the surrounding natural terrain. This barn is listed in the National Historic Register. ©2003 Keith Baum, Coolstock.com

other farm structures. Scenes of stately horses, herds of cattle, and other favorite farm animals are common themes for the sides of barns. Each image has its own story to tell and often serves to relate the likes and dislikes of its owners. Sometimes it simply covers up the fading remnants of a long-since faded advertising billboard.

The Pennsylvania-German–style bank barn proved its usefulness over time and needs no promotion. The American farmer has been sold on the practical advantages of a multiple-story structure that takes advantage of the surrounding land, provides an inherently easy form of access, and helps shelter animals with an open overhang. Today this influence is evident by the number of working bank barns seen throughout North America.

Whether they're called Pennsylvania-German barns, Pennsylvania Dutch barns, or even Pennsylvania Deutsch barns, these farm-friendly structures share a common denominator of innovation and ingenuity. When it comes to these barns, function and forebay are one in the same.

The restored "Star Barn" near Harrisburg, Pennsylvania, incorporates Gothic-influenced ventilation treatments with the overhanging laube found on the typical bank barn. This melding of styles, combined with the addition of a star-shaped vent at center, creates a beautiful effect. ©2003 Keith Baum, Coolstock.com

On the American family farm, honey, eggs, and other homegrown products are often sold on the side to provide a steady revenue stream for enterprising farmers. ©2003 Keith Baum, Coolstock.com

The repeating sheaves of wheat pattern incorporated into this brick-end bank barn in Lititz, Pennsylvania, were added to provide a practical means of ventilating the stored hay as well as to please the eye.
©2003 Keith Baum, Coolstock.com

This barn mural in Elizabethtown, Pennsylvania, is sponsored by the local insurance company and recalls the harvest of the 1920s—a time when steam-powered tractors were a common sight on the well-equipped American farm. ©2003 Keith Baum, Coolstock.com

After Benjamin Franklin enlightened people about the idiosyncrasies of lightning, rooftop lightning rods were installed on countless barns to provide protection. Historic Rock Ford in Lancaster, Pennsylvania, is the home for this wood-and-brick masterpiece. ©2003 Keith Baum, Coolstock.com

The massive wood beams that support the cantilevered extension of this stone-foundation bank barn recall a time when large timbers were a staple commodity. ©2003 Keith Baum, Coolstock.com

Chapter Three

English Barn

Design and Austerity

If different barn types were represented by flavors, the English variety would most certainly be vanilla. In terms of design and function, a barn doesn't come any more basic than this. Known in different regions of the United States and Canada as the "Yankee," "Connecticut," or the "three-bay" barn, the English barn exists as one of the earliest forms of architecture imported to North America by the first colonists.

As architectural history shows, features of the English barn hark back to the farm buildings of the Elizabethan Age, a time when the agricultural economy was dominated by the cultivation and harvest of wheat. During the era when food (and alcoholic beverages) made from grain sustained the masses, there was a great need for a utilitarian shelter that enabled farmers to process hay, store grain, and repair tools. The English barn was a style that satisfied all of these requirements quite adequately.

The configuration saw such widespread use that even the English government issued its stamp of approval. In 1798, the *British Report on Agriculture* published plans detailing how to build a Spartan barn. The report emphasized the barn's modesty and referred to it as a "Small English Barn." It was tacit confirmation that this was the kind of barn that the English farmer should build, and it was a nod to centuries of real-world testing and day-to-day use.

Stewart Creek, Michigan, is a long way from New England, but not far enough away to escape the subtle influences of original American architecture. Here two gambrel-roof barns are combined into one and join gable side entry to eaves. ©2003 Keith Baum, Coolstock.com

Sunrise in Brownstown, Pennsylvania, reveals multiple rooftop ventilators and a grain storage silo—two essentials for any style of American barn. ©2003 Keith Baum, Coolstock.com

This style of barn was a do-it-yourself project within the reach of any farmer who could afford a few loads of bricks and the services of a mason. Carpentry work was minimal, and the architectural features didn't require the mastery of difficult building techniques. The style did without windows, porches, cupolas, and a myriad of other accoutrements that amplified the image of the barn during the coming centuries. It was believed that if a feature didn't contribute to utility, there was no reason to go through the trouble and expense to include it.

The basic English barn was a no-frills workhorse and was defined by a few distinct features. Its characteristic rectangular shape was laid out in a proportion of 2-to-1, with a footprint of approximately 25 by 55 feet. The roof was a typical gable variety with triangular panels that topped each end.

The British plan had a continuous ridge roof set at a shallow pitch that was covered with long wooden planks or slate. In contrast, the more elaborate barns of Europe sported roofs made entirely of thatch and pitched at an angle of 45 degrees or more. Through the ages, it was discovered that bundled reeds shed rain water more effectively when roofs were built this way.

The foundation design was slightly less refined. At the time, most of the barns that followed the English model had no formal foundation as we know it today. The sills were laid on individual stone footings, or underpinnings. The sill ran the entire length and width of the building to provide a place to tie in the frame and exterior

Opposite: When commercially manufactured metal sheathing became available, barn builders used it to replace more traditional materials. This abandoned barn in Anna, Illinois, shows how even durable metal can deteriorate. ©2003 Howard Ande, Coolstock.com

siding. Later, many barns were built with excavated, basement-type foundations, while others were anchored to low walls.

Despite the austerity of the stone foundation, uncomplicated roof, and straightforward frame, the plan managed to exude a sense of simple elegance. The arched entryway caught one's eye as did the vertically oriented, double diamond-shaped patterns of ventilation holes that straddled the entryways. Specific bricks were purposely left out during construction to provide an unrestricted flow of air through the structure. This same novel ventilation feature later resurfaced in the great barns in Pennsylvania.

One could say that access to the English barn was also unrestricted. In fact, a convenient point of ingress and egress was integral to the overall design. A large opening was positioned at the center of each eaves-side. Inside, the space was divided into three separate compartments, and the center bay was aligned with both of the doors.

With spacing between the boards, horizontal slats provide the pass-through ventilation required for curing hay. ©2003 Howard Ande, Coolstock.com

51

Bank barns combine the eaves-side entry accessibility of the classic English barn with the storage capabilities of multiple-level barns. ©2003 Ron Saari, Coolstock.com

The side-entry, English bank barn, with raised berm to allow entry, combines a simple rectangular floor plan with a stout foundation and wall treatment of natural stone. ©2003 Ron Saari, Coolstock.com

Larger bays to the left and right were used to store hay and grain. A small compartment built into the side of one bay provided a holding bin to store the sheaves that awaited processing. Tools and other implements were also stored along the walls of this central, pass-through bay.

The threshing (pronounced thrashing) floor, or center compartment, was the most important component of the design. This bay functioned as the farmer's main work area and was used during various stages of the harvest. In terms of size, the space was large enough for a horse-drawn wagon, and eventually a tractor, to pull in, deliver loads, and move about the room.

The Yankee barns of Washington, Vermont, are evidence of the English influence. This gable-entry barn follows the connected plan and is attached to the adjoining farmhouse at the opposite gable end. ©2003 Ron Saari, Coolstock.com

The structure also enabled the farmer to exit efficiently. When the job was done, the farmer marched the team of horses forward and directly out the other side. An identical doorway installed in the opposite wall provided one of the earliest forms of drive-in, drive-out convenience.

With the wagon clear, the threshing floor was used to process the harvested stalks of wheat, barley, rye, or buckwheat. The procedure was simple but labor intensive. First, the stalks were beaten to loosen the seed or corn from the stems. After the heads of grain were separated, the husks were winnowed by tossing basketfuls of grain into the air. When the right technique was used, the wind did all of the work to separate the chaff from the kernels. At the door base, a raised length of wood across the opening held the falling grain inside. This is the origin of the word threshold, a term still used when referring to the piece of hardwood that forms the bottom of a doorway.

Gradually a few of the barn's impractical features were changed. New Englanders came to the conclusion that the traditional placement of doors under the eaves wasn't conducive to year-round operation. During the winter, the heavy accumulation of snow on the roof usually slid off into a large pile that blocked

Back in the days before electricity, oil lamps were used to provide light in the flammable interior of the barn. ©2003 Keith Baum, Coolstock.com

Five rooftop cupolas with accompanying lightning rods grace the roof of this fading red, end drive barn in Danforth, Illinois. ©2003 Howard Ande, Coolstock.com

Barn doors positioned on the eaves side were typical of the English barn prototype, such as this Gettysburg, Pennsylvania, survivor. *©2003 Keith Baum, Coolstock.com*

Near Dixon, Illinois, farming operations are falling under the storm clouds of change, as they are in many other American farming regions. As architectural styles change, so do the business models that once supported them. *©2003 Howard Ande, Coolstock.com*

Hillside farm structures like this Waitsfield, Vermont, barn were often oriented so the entryway was positioned on the gable end. This model allows easy access into the basement level from the lower part of the hill. ©2003 Howard Ande, Coolstock.com

access. Barn builders found a simple solution. They moved the doors from the sides and installed them in the gable ends. Thus, the subtle architectural variation known as the Yankee barn was born.

At the same time, adjustments were made to address the availability of local materials. When the first New England colonies were settled, virgin forests provided what appeared to be an endless inventory of low-cost building stock. With an ample supply of timber, there was little conjecture over what material to use. Wood was the logical choice over brick or stone, which were heavy and more expensive to transport over long distances.

Taking these factors into account, builders relied on heavy timbers and careful carpentry to construct the barn frame. The large wooden supports were cut entirely from tree trunks. To shape them into usable beams, builders hewed the supports with a broad axe. Then a hoe-like tool called an adze was used to smooth the rough surface. The hewer straddled the log and swung the tool between his legs. Gradually wood was chipped away to create rectangular posts and beams. In later years, the laborious process of hand-crafting beams was assumed by the steel blade of the sawmill.

It would be a number of years before any machine could reduce the time it took to fit together a frame. Joining timbers to build a barn of great structural integrity

Pot-bellied pigs and barnyard cats are two types of domesticated creatures that are routinely found on the American farm. ©2003 Keith Baum, Coolstock.com

The rooftop cupola provided ventilation to the haymow and a certain amount of natural light to the interior. In an age before electricity, windows were the only means to bring light into a structure. ©2003 Keith Baum, Coolstock.com

remained a core skill of the carpenter's craft. For now, it was work that could only be done by hand. When building the frame, each joint required a pocket that was cut into the beam, or mortise. The mating beam required a corresponding tenon, or protrusion that fit into the mortise. Using the centuries-old scribe rule technique, joiners cut each tenon to fit a specific mortise in the frame.

The concept was simple to understand, but the technique wasn't easy to master. First, the mortise was cut to shape. Then, a hand-powered auger was used to drill out the first bits of wood. At this stage, the rough pocket was cut to shape with a large chisel and mallet. Then, the receiving timber, the one that was intended to mate with this mortise, was paired up with the cutout and scribed according to the overlaying outline. The tenon was then shaped by chiseling away the excess wood up to the scribe line. Finally, the two ends slipped together.

To give the workers something to go by when erecting the frame, marriage marks were inscribed on the outside faces of the beams. These Roman–numeral-like glyphs made the barn frame easy to put together and couldn't be seen after the frame was put together. The marks helped turn the project into the equivalent of a build-it-by-the-numbers erector set.

Conversely, a process known as the "square rule" was adopted around the early 1800s. This technique also yielded stout framing results, although it relied less on

When the American colonies were first settled, Finger Lakes, New York, was a region under English influence. Today a variety of barn types flourish there, including decaying structures like this gambrel roof example. ©2003 Keith Baum, Coolstock.com

the precision needed to join together two unique pieces. In this case, the ends of the timbers were shaped from patterns and precise measurements and marked with a specially made jig called a framing square. Because each joint was made to match a master pattern, barn builders spent less time custom-fitting and trimming the timbers. Only when the barn was raised would the joints be checked for fit (and then adjusted, if necessary).

For the exterior walls, two forms of sheathing were used for the siding. Clapboards were either nailed in a horizontal pattern to the exterior studs, or planks were attached in a vertically oriented arrangement. Small gaps were left between the planks to allow air circulation. In both cases, the boards covered the frame until nearly down to the ground level. Because of the close proximity of the siding to the bottom of the sill, it was important for the foundation to be slightly higher than the site terrain. Otherwise, termites and standing water would quickly rot the wood.

To protect the entire barn from the damaging effects of the elements, the roof and its accompanying support structure was built to withstand punishment. Barn builders used a variety of techniques to achieve stability, such as adding the architectural element known as the truss. Designed in a number of configurations, roof

We've come a long way since the settlement of New England. Today the American family farmstead is slipping into obscurity. As factory farms and global conglomerates seize the market, scenes like this are more difficult to find. ©2003 Bruce Leighty, Coolstock.com

These Komoka, Ontario, storage barns feature large, side-entry doors to store firewood. ©2003 Keith Baum, Coolstock.com

trusses of the day were essentially a triangle of joined timbers with added support elements. King-post trusses featured one interior support, and queen-post trusses had two supports. A series of these trusses rested on the plates of a barn frame (the horizontal timbers located at the top of the walls) to distribute the weight of the roof throughout the entire structure.

Overhead, trusses supported a series of rafters and adjoining purlins. Here wooden shingles or stone tiles replaced the more archaic thatched materials and added substantial weight. Oddly enough, the English pattern of gentle pitch—or one-third as it was described in the parlance of the carpenter—remained the standard. It's interesting to note that the steep roof that sometimes identifies a barn

as the English variety exists merely as a throwback to the early thatched roofing materials. In terms of overall usability or function, it serves no purpose when covered with conventional shingles.

By the 1850s, the interior of the English barn evolved into a space with even more purpose. At that time, the economic focus of American agriculture moved away from the production of grain and began to focus on the raising and managing of livestock. To accommodate this paradigm shift, the architecture of the English grain barn was melded with the design rationale of the American livestock stable. "The barn," as many referred to it, emerged as a hybrid structure that housed livestock operations with threshing and crop storage under a single roof. Now it was a multi-purpose, multitasking facility that galloped boldly toward the future.

The prosperous farming operations that could invest the extra capital led the parade. The remodeling of existing barns came first, followed by the construction of super-sized models that were big from the ground up. Meanwhile, other farmers realized the extra space they wanted was right under their feet. To make room for the collection and storage of manure, basements were dug out. In many instances, a barn was made larger by moving or building an adjacent second barn. When that

In Dearborn, Michigan, Greenfield Village has preserved many architectural artifacts that might have been lost. A seventeenth-century, English stone barn with accompanying storage tower is one of many attractions. ©2003 Keith Baum, Coolstock.com

Lancaster, Pennsylvania, is home to a variety of barns grown from a variety of ancestral roots. Bank barns, with their walls and foundations built completely of stone, have been able to withstand the ravages of time and bridge the gap between the old world and the new. ©2003 Keith Baum, Coolstock.com

option wasn't feasible, a lean-to slapped together with recycled lumber provided a quick, low-budget alternative.

In the end, the changes became established practices, and barns emerged on a much larger scale. Some stretched to 60 feet or more in length. Of course, this extension equated to an abundance of additional square footage inside, most notably on the threshing floor. In North America, farmers used this interior bonus space to undertake expanded threshing activities and store farm implements.

Key to the propagation of this expanded design was a structural element called a swing beam. Incorporated into the building's superstructure, it was designed to support an extra floor over the threshing floor, one that could be installed and removed on demand. When the harvest exceeded expectations, farmers slipped the ends of floor joists (which were stored away) into precut holes in the swing beam. Once the temporary floorboards were laid into place, the new loft stored extra fodder.

Innovation like this pulled farming closer in sync with the changing times. As advances in agriculture spawned by the Industrial Revolution collided with tradition, new construction techniques and technologies were considered. Against the cry of the traditionalists, proponents of a more refined design aesthetic moved to update commercial, domestic, and agricultural architecture. "Farmers should be put on guard against laying out extravagant sums for the sake of making their barns 'artistic' and elegant structures," warned architect J. H. Hammond in 1858. "We have contended that decorations are useless on a dwelling-house; they are utterly senseless on

Near Lancaster, Pennsylvania, this graphic barn mural recalls the time when America's English, Dutch, and German settlers made their way out West to establish a new life and claim the free land that was offered. ©2003 Keith Baum, Coolstock.com

63

When stone reigned as the building material for barns, storage silos were not yet in widespread use. Grain was often stored in a separate bay within the barn. ©2003 Keith Baum, Coolstock.com

a barn." Nevertheless, the Victorian design aesthetic, with its applied decorative embellishments, began to make inroads.

For good or bad, new decorative elements were added into the mix of barn design. Down on the farm, things were definitely changing, as evidenced by board-and-batten siding, decorative window trim, bracketed cornices, and fancy cupolas.

By the dawn of the nineteenth century, the barn that began with simple aspirations had changed to satisfy the demands of the work placed upon it as well as the creative aspirations and dreams of the farmers who owned it. The metamorphosis was complete. Once upon a time, the English barn was considered plain vanilla, but now, the "30-by-40" was a practical tool, a boon to the evolution of agriculture, and an important component of the American dream.

This barn at Lafayette's headquarters at the Historic Brandywine Battlefield in Chadds Ford, Pennsylvania, harkens back to a time when the English battled the colonials to win control of New England. ©2003 Keith Baum, Coolstock.com

The influence of colonial architecture is greatest in the regions in and around New England. Here it is common to find tidy, connected barn arrangements with all the trappings of the well-planned farmstead. *©2003 Keith Baum, Coolstock.com*

The Gothic connotation of the rainbow-style roof recalls the shapes and patterns of church interiors found in Old World England and other parts of Europe. For the American farmer, the spacious configuration provided the extra storage needed to feed a growing herd. ©2003 Keith Baum, Coolstock.com

Colonial-inspired dormers, rooftop ventilators, a side garage, and an overhanging porch combine into one plan and form a distinctive hybrid. ©2003 Keith Baum, Coolstock.com

67

Chapter Four

Round Barn

A Circular Simplicity

During the 1960s, prominent architect Bertram Goldberg paid tribute 100 years of unorthodox building plans when he rebelled against what he called "the engineer's module applied to society." Lending long-overdue credence to the generations of hardscrabble builders who had gone before him, he suggested that rectilinear shapes were opposed to human activities. Circular buildings, he argued, better served activity and helped foster a sense of community.

Goldberg's reasoning was based on three important points: circular buildings provide more efficient wind resistance, they enable more direct mechanical distribution, and they offer more usable interior square footage. The widespread adoption of the circular configuration by numerous cultures around the world has shown that he was right.

Why must a building—a barn for that matter—be constructed with four corners and an angular, pitched roof? Architects, agriculturalists, and scholars have debated the question since humans first built structures used to house families, store food, and shelter livestock. Down through the ages, the circle has provided inspiration and practical advantages to the architects of countless structures, barns included.

As far back as 4000 B.C., China's Neolithic Yangshao culture embraced the organic shape of the circle for its sunken, mud-and-grass dwellings. During the Bronze Age, the people who inhabited the European continent

Round barns, like the type seen in Burnet, Vermont, were once prevalent in the New England area. Forward-thinking farmers welcomed round architecture as a practical alternative to the rectangular plan.

69

©2003 Howard Ande, Coolstock.com

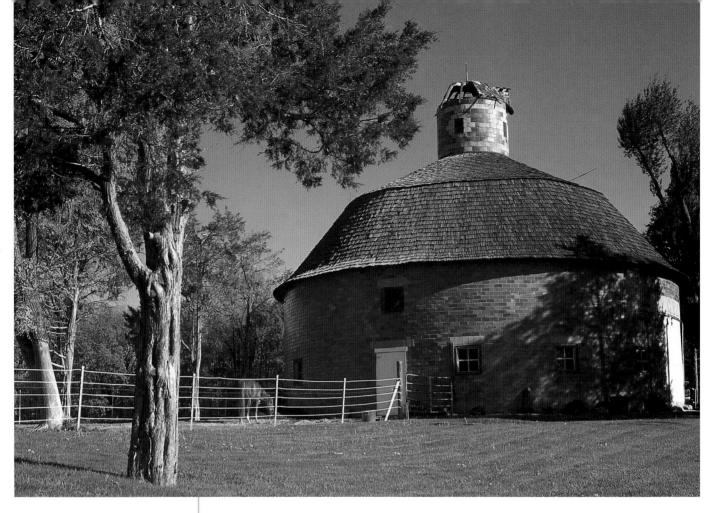

The round barn near Angola, Indiana, incorporates brown tile for its shell. Tile, which was popularized between the 1910s and 1920s, provided barn builders a durable substitute for wood. ©2003 Keith Baum, Coolstock.com

constructed round houses made from rounded boulders. On the North American continent, the Inuits exploited the structural advantages of the circle for their igloos. Further south, the Wampanoag Indians also built their dwellings with the circle as guide. Their buildings were covered with mats and thus were easily transported to another location.

To this day, native cultures continue to build in the round. In the tropical forests of Guyana, the indigenous WaiWai people construct circular huts that symbolize different aspects of their cosmological beliefs. Inside these large, cone-shaped dwellings, a succession of horizontal planes conceptualizes specific areas of the universe. Carefully placed apertures in the roof represent passageways to the cosmos. Here even the rafters and purlins hold significance and correspond to specific cosmological spaces. The area that surrounds the central structural support, or hub, is viewed as sacred space and is surrounded by the various WaiWai households.

History proves this mystical reverence for geometry, and its influence upon architecture, isn't unique to any one race or culture. The Greek philosopher

Aristotle considered the circle to be the perfect shape. The circle represented the computation of pi, or the ratio of the circumference to the diameter, to mathematician Archimedes. To the Shakers, a religious sect that emigrated from England in 1774 to pursue their religious freedom in America, the circle was both divine and scientific.

According to barn historians Eric Arthur and Dudley Whitney, authors of *The Barn: A Vanishing Landmark in North America*, the Shakers displayed admiration for the circle and incorporated the shape into many of their everyday objects. They used the circle in their inspirational drawings and incorporated it into the repeating, geometric patterns of their quilts. When they weren't fashioning round hats, rugs, and boxes for sale or personal use, they crafted round drawer pulls and handrests to adorn their furniture. These items were a dramatic contrast to the Shakers' extremely angular furniture.

The interior framework of the Angola, Indiana, round barn demonstrates just how sound circular construction methods could be. Note the intricate structural lattice. ©2003 Keith Baum, Coolstock.com

The Shakers' most spectacular tribute to the circle was constructed in 1826, when the community in Hancock, Massachusetts, crafted an immense round barn from native wood and stone. Defined by their communal style of living, the Shakers had a distinct advantage when it came to building large, functional structures used for farming purposes. They had a ready labor force at their disposal and an affinity for community cooperation, both of which helped them execute big projects quickly. When it came to raising barns and building community structures, the Shakers made their mark on the architectural landscape with several ambitious projects on their principle communes in Massachusetts, New Hampshire, New York, and Ohio, including some significant examples of bank barns.

Compared to the typical style of barn architecture that ruled the day, the Shakers' entry into the realm of circular barn construction was unorthodox but extremely well designed. Classified as an experimental barn in Richard Rawson's *Old Barn Plans*, a careful perusal of the floor and cross-section views of this expansive structure illustrates that this building was designed for every possible contingency. The design was not an experimental one by any means. It was a plan that took into account sound building practices and the ultimate use for the finished structure.

The curved interior of this round barn in West Bloomfield, Michigan, provides an excellent sense of space. Many such barns have found a new purpose and have been converted into homes. ©2003 Keith Baum, Coolstock.com

The double doors and natural river rock of this round barn, which was converted to a residence in West Bloomfield, Michigan, recall an age when meticulous stone masons took pride in their work. ©2003 Keith Baum, Coolstock.com

The Shaker plan took full advantage of stone for the barn superstructure and didn't rely on heavy wood timbers and the standard techniques of framing. Unlike the construction of a straight wall, which often required careful planning to prevent it from toppling, the circular foundation laid down by the Shaker stone masons didn't demand any special fortification. Two courses of stone, one used for strength and the other for exterior finish, combined to create a 25-foot-high wall rigid enough to stand without the aid of a buttress. By interlocking stones around the circumference, the Shakers demonstrated one of the most important principles of circular design: structural integrity.

Numerous paned window openings were strategically positioned throughout the ashlar-patterned stone wall to provide light to the interior cattle stalls. Doored passageways allowed access to the interior. Inside the building, the outermost part of the wheel was reserved for a functional driveway, which was 15 feet wide. Here wagons moved freely around the circumference to service the facilities in the center.

A secondary, shed-like addition protruded up from the flat roof like a layer on a cake. Known as a monitor roof, this feature provided natural light to illuminate the haymow and interior space. Supplementary ventilation was supplied by surrounding

Because windows were difficult to incorporate into the curved wall of round barns, openings were traditionally small and modest.
©2003 Keith Baum, Coolstock.com

clerestory windows, functional openings that had their origins in the imposing architecture and stained-glass windows typical of the classical churches of England.

An ornate cupola at the center of this monitor roof provided the majority of airflow for the structure. It was part of an octagonal-shaped central shaft that ran all the way up through the hub of the building. Smartly outfitted with its own array of windows (other variations employed slatted openings or louvers) and topped with a weather vane to indicate wind direction, the cupola was one of the earliest forms of natural air conditioning. When the wind blew across the openings, the drop in air pressure created a suction vortex and drew air up and out from the cavity below without the aid of electrical fans or other equipment.

Improved ventilation is yet another reason why building a round barn is advantageous. All farmers know that proper barn airflow is necessary for safety since wet hay generates a certain amount of heat, and spontaneous combustion can quickly ignite a fire. Fire prevention requires a little bit of common sense, but the practice of storing hay is a learned art. The farmer must make sure the hay is dry enough to store, but not so dry that the leaves shatter off when it is handled. This wasn't always an easy task, since forecasting the weather in the days before long-range Doppler radar and global positioning satellites wasn't that straightforward. Farmers were guided by printed almanacs, word of mouth, superstition, and other historical data to enhance the monitoring and anticipation of changing climatic conditions.

The structural framework of round barns is inherently more stable than the traditional skeleton of other barns. This integrity also brings a definite aura of architectural beauty.
©2003 Keith Baum, Coolstock.com

During the early 1800s, the state-of-the-art forecasting tools were weather vanes. In America, the early colonists took great delight in adorning their meeting halls and public buildings with vanes, or *fanes* as they were originally called. The term *fane* comes from the Anglo-Saxon word meaning "flag," which referred to the fabric pennants used in medieval Europe to show archers wind direction.

The round barn in Old Fort, Pennsylvania, demonstrates just how extensive circular architecture can be. This multistoried design features a rooftop cupola, extensive ventilation louvers, and an ample array of windows. ©2003 Ron Saari, Coolstock.com.

Americans were soon hooked on weather vanes, particularly those with patriotic designs. The Goddess of Liberty and the Federal Eagle were popular models. By the 1850s, weather vanes of famous racing horses such as Black Hawk and Smuggler made their way to the rooftops. They were modeled after the Currier and Ives prints that bore their likenesses.

As weather vanes spun about in the breeze, news of the Shakers' round barn spread to all points on the compass. "The round barn is beginning to have a place on some of the biggest farms in New England," reported John E. Taylor in the April 1914 issue of the *Breeder's Gazette*. "J. L. Dean, of Maine, has built one that has cost less than a rectangular, and he finds it more practical."

Forward-thinking agrarians in New England and other parts of the country allowed themselves to think outside of the box and built round barns. Wood timber versions of the Shaker round barn made their way as far west as the Great Plains, and some appeared in Kansas, Nebraska, and the Dakotas. Other variants were constructed with stone, brick, and clay tile.

This round barn in West Bloomfield, Michigan, provides many examples of the metalworking craftsmanship that once prevailed. The art of creating tools, implements, and utilitarian objects was part of the farmer's tasks 100 years ago. ©2003 Keith Baum, Coolstock.com

Round barns are often constructed in geometric expressions, such as the octagon. This decaying structure was most likely used for hay or feed storage. ©2003 Keith Baum, Coolstock.com

Clay tiles first made their way into the annals of barn history between 1910 and 1918. During that time, proponents of agriculture wanted to cultivate the poorly drained area of north-central Iowa known as the prairie pothole region. This section of the state boasted some of the most fertile soils in the world, but the area was largely unused due to the geology of the region. In an effort to reclaim the land, the water was drained, and the clay was excavated. Based on this new resource, Iowa emerged as

America's leading producer of drainage tile. So much tile was manufactured that new construction methods emerged.

The first efforts to incorporate hollow clay tile into the standard framework of commercial architecture were initiated by the agricultural college in Ames, Iowa. Practical experiments resulted in the construction of structures suitable for farming, including storage silos, corn cribs, and barns. Because tiles could be formed to fit around a circumference with little effort, they were particularly well-suited for the construction of circular designs. According to historical records, 180 of the more than 100,000 barns built in Iowa between 1830 and 1940 were round. Many of these were characterized by hollow clay tiles.

A self-supporting roof was another attribute that defined many of the round barns being built in Iowa and other areas of the country, and its inclusion was another reason why the round barn was superior. Structural support was inherent to a conically

A roof defined by two distinct pitches could be called a gambrel, unless it is applied in a round barn like this one in Oskaloosa, Kansas. *©2003 Ron Saari, Coolstock.com*

The residents of Elgin, Illinois, recognize this local landmark as a 16-sided barn, a rare example that provides storage and space for modern farming activities. ©2003 Howard Ande, Coolstock.com

The circle has inspired much of the architecture and many of the tools found on the American farm, including grain storage silos and windmills. Note the dinner bell mounted in the cupola. ©2003 Keith Baum, Coolstock.

shaped roof. The rafters radiated downward from a central apex to eliminate the need for additional purlins (the horizontal roof beams that normally added support to the rafters). In terms of stability, this characteristic provided a design that was inherently stronger than standard, pitched roof construction, and had gables positioned on both ends.

Without a web of internal supports to bear the load of the roof, the amount of storage space inside a barn increased. The circular form provided greater volume-to-surface ratio than the rectangular form. Multiple barn buildings could be combined into a single structure and occupy less land. Because of the increased amount of square footage, there was no need to back equipment out of a corner in a round barn. Cleanup was simplified, too. The lack of right angles and corners that normally accumulated dirt translated into less sweeping.

In regards to everyday maintenance, saving time was a great benefit since many of the earliest round barns were built with three levels, which almost tripled the amount of upkeep. In most instances, the top floor was used as a haymow to allow feed to be delivered by way of the hollow center pylon or to be pulled down over the parapet into the open area below. On the middle floor, stanchions positioned around the circumference accommodated a great number of cows for feeding or milking. The basement level stored manure. It was easily shoveled through trap doors and was later hauled out by wagon or cart.

This octagonal Waitsfield, Vermont, barn, complete with circular rooftop cupola and weather vane, has been fully restored. It has become a well-known and familiar roadside site. ©2003 Howard Ande, Coolstock.com

The central hub that was originally used for ventilation was soon modified for other purposes. By the 1890s, farmers moved away from using the underground pits to store silage and began to build vertical silos inside their barns to store fodder. The corners were often boarded on the diagonal to avoid spoilage and create a more circular storage space inside. With this in mind, it seemed logical to replace the center hub of the round barn with more useable storage, particularly for feed. This was a boon

With a flared roof and complement of lower windows, this round barn in Manhatten, Illinois, has incorporated a circular storage silo at its center. ©2003 Bruce Leighty, Coolstock.com

to dairy farmers since fodder could be supplied to the herd year round and would allow cows to be milked during the winter months. Hauling feed from pits was a bygone chore. Now gravity delivered hay to exactly where it was needed without additional effort or need to move the herd.

Taking this and other features into consideration, it was clear that the round barn was a viable and cost-effective alternative to the standard iteration. In 1912, an American agricultural report confirmed this sentiment when it summed up the advantages of the round barn in three words: convenience, strength, and cheapness. It went on to report that it featured a large, unobstructed hayloft, and estimated the cost of building a round barn to be as much as 58 percent less than that of a traditional rectangular barn.

Whether it was determined by cultural preference, religious reverence, or the strict attention to practical advantages, a farmer's choice to build in the round was supported by more than just the quest for beautiful aesthetics. Round barns assumed a special place in the history of American agricultural architecture. Today one may still find surviving examples in all regions of the country. Some may be in their natural, derelict state; others have been restored to their original splendor. Many have been reopened to the public as historical museums, bed and breakfasts, and restaurants, and a handful have been remodeled into homes. The barns stand proudly as a reminder of good old American ingenuity and are a testament to those who had the pluck and determination to march to the beat of a different drummer.

"They built them round so the devil couldn't corner you," said the early American settlers of the round barns that sprouted up across the verdant fields of the New World. While that explanation may or may not have been true, it is certain that they built the barns round to be different, make a statement that building practices don't always need to coincide with the status quo, and prove circular architecture is just as at home on the farm as it is in other areas of commercial architecture.

This extended-plan round barn near Seward, Illinois, takes on the appearance of a massive ship, complete with rooftop cupolas, overhanging porches, and connected service structures. ©2003 Howard Ande, Coolstock.com

Motorists driving west of Chicago, Illinois, may still spy an occasional barn with a rooftop cupola and a weather vane. However, a witch riding a broom is a much rarer sight. ©2003 Howard Ande, Coolstock.com

Round or rectangular, a barn's charm sometimes lies in the exterior trim details surrounding the doors, windows, and other architectural features. ©2003 Keith Baum, Coolstock.com

The Whistle Stop Park in Colmer, Pennsylvania, is the place to visit when looking for an eight-side, or octagon barn. This example incorporates the structural integrity of a stone foundation with the flexibility of a wood frame. ©2003 Ron Saari, Coolstock.com

Still in everyday use, this Michigan octagon barn incorporates an unusual layer-cake design. It showcases dormer windows in the middle level, a windowed cupola on the upper level, and an octagonal mounting base for the metal ventilator. ©2003 Keith Baum, Coolstock.com

The unique wagon wheel, overhead sliding-track door treatment of the Angola, Indiana, round barn demonstrates how difficult it is to mate rectangular doors with a circular structure. ©2003 Keith Baum, Coolstock.com

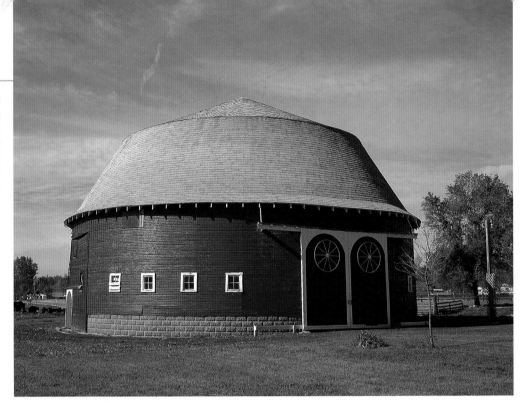

The colonial-inspired features of this Bryan, Ohio, octagon barn give the structure more of a domestic feel than is usually portrayed in a building used for commercial farming activities. ©2003 Keith Baum, Coolstock.com

Built with substantial materials and considerable care, barns such as this Michigan circular model are often converted into businesses. ©2003 *Keith Baum, Coolstock.com*

The pointed, high-peaked roof of this smaller octagon barn, located near Adamstown, Pennsylvania, stirs up visions of Europe's medieval castles and thatched-roof structures. ©2003 Keith Baum, Coolstock.com

At Corn State College in Pennsylvania, students may experience firsthand the majesty that is the round barn. In models such as this, animals were housed in the lower level, and hay was stored in the upper mow. ©2003 Keith Baum, Coolstock.com

Chapter Five

American Barn

Pride of the Prairies

In 1862, President Abraham Lincoln signed the Homestead Act, one of the most important pieces of legislation in the history of the United States. Large tracts of open land were thrust into the public domain and offered to private citizens. There were 270 million acres available, an area that comprised almost 10 percent of the entire country.

To claim a 160-acre parcel of land and make it their own, homesteaders had to meet three requirements: be at least 21 years old, be the head of a household, and be solvent enough to pay an $18 filing fee. The remainder of the obligation was to be paid out in sweat equity. In order to gain title and a legal patent to the land, homesteaders had to build a house (and a barn if possible), make improvements, and live on it for five years.

While future land barons packed their saddlebags, Congress voted to approve a charter to the Union Pacific Railroad, which had already begun the construction of a steam train line that headed west from Council Bluffs, Iowa. Meanwhile, the Central Pacific Railroad was laying down some tracks of its own, shooting a line of steel and cross-ties east from Sacramento, California.

On May 10, 1869, telegraph keys clicked out the message to newspapers around the country that the two lines had finally met. For a short while, Utah's Promontory Point was the epicenter of the world. The time

The twin silos that accompany the barn structures of this Oregon, Pennsylvania, dairy barn are evidence there are many cattle here that require feeding. ©2003 Keith Baum, Coolstock.com

it took to travel across the country was reduced from months to days. "Go west, young man" was the phrase on everyone's lips, and many people heeded the call.

With a world of opportunities unfolding, newly arrived immigrants joined those already established in contemplation of this once-in-a-lifetime chance to own your own farmstead. As fast as they could pack up their belongings and harness their animals, bands of rugged individualists pointed horses and prairie schooners (Conestoga wagons) toward the setting sun and forged a trail westward to stake their claim on the free land.

Farmers of every nationality crossed the Mason-Dixon Line and the Mississippi River to plant the seeds of a new life in the valleys of Virginia, grasslands of Missouri, plains of Kansas, and places even further beyond. One farmstead at a time, the frontier was pushed back and civilized. The formerly unpopulated gap of land between the East and West Coast (communities of Native Americans notwithstanding) was redefined by surveyors' tools and lines on a map.

The sun sets on this substantial farming operation in Leola, Pennsylvania. Oversized twin barns, silo, and a farmhouse are evidence that this farmer is more than just a weekend gardener. ©2003 Keith Baum, Coolstock.com

The barn made its way across the prairies, too. It changed and evolved to adapt to the new terrain and uses that lay ahead. This was a pivotal time in the history of American barns, as the population shift toward the West spawned a myriad of architectural variations—each one conformed to a unique need and requirement. The culturally influenced architecture born on the European continent was no longer applicable. The barn was merged, modified, and updated to meet the expectations of new lifestyles and modes of farming.

Gradually, raising and selling cattle for meat and dairy production gained momentum, and the resulting commodities replaced wheat, tobacco, and cotton as the nation's primary agricultural products. Cattlemen joined the rush of settlers and made claims of their own. The fertile grasslands that stretched from Texas to the upper Missouri River were ideal grazing lands and were the perfect places to feed and raise immense herds of Longhorn cattle.

Sprawling cattle ranches soon appeared in places such as the Dakota territory, Wyoming, Colorado, Nebraska, and Kansas. To satisfy the nation's increasing

The corn crib is a variation of the barn used to store feed. These cribs in Paradise, Pennsylvania, are fully loaded. ©2003 Keith Baum, Coolstock.com

When settlers moved west, they took the building styles derived from early prototypes in Europe with them. This end-drive barn design uses the weather-resistant woods indigenous to the Western states. ©2003 Howard Ande, Coolstock.com

White is an appropriate exterior color for dairy barns, as shown by this Amish example found in Leola, Pennsylvania. The production of milk is an extremely clean process and requires a stringent adherence to cleanliness and quality control. ©2003 Keith Baum, Coolstock.com

appetite for beef, pork, and other meat products, slaughter houses and meat processing plants became big businesses. Packing meat for shipment and sale turned from art to science. Almost overnight, small cities and rustic cow towns were transformed into prominent commercial hubs.

As populations shifted, the wide-open West—and the boundary-free land that started it all—wasn't so wide-open anymore. In 20 years, countless homestead claims, miles of barbed-wire fences, and the increasing number of railroad tracks contributed to the end of the cross-country cattle drives. Eventually serious ranchers had their own land on which to raise their herds. As a result, the need for a special barn was needed; its attributes were dictated by the requirement to feed livestock around the clock, 365 days year. This was the beginning of the so-called Western barn, a wooden edifice that focused on aiding the process of raising and maintaining the livestock.

When settlers first landed in North America, cattle were slaughtered before winter, since the task of feeding them and keeping them alive throughout the cold season was more than a full-time job. The farmers in the milder West and Southwest

A rainbow roof, in combination with side shed protrusions, dramatically extends the ground-level working space of this Lancaster, Pennsylvania, barn. ©2003 Keith Baum, Coolstock.com

didn't have to worry much about sheltering animals from snow and freezing temperatures so the emphasis of their barns shifted from the byre and onto the mow.

Barns adapted in size and height to accommodate the increased amount of feed. Long, sweeping roof coverings marked the prairie barn and provided an extended amount of storage room inside, similar to the roof of the Dutch barn. At the front ridge, some roofs projected slightly outward to form a kind of triangular "beak," an addition that had two purposes. Wagon doors on the ground level and the hay door one floor above were protected from the rain. More important, the addition of this structural element marked the point of attachment for a projecting arm that held the hay carrier pulley assembly.

A hay carrier was a clever combination of wheels, pulleys, and latches that made the task of moving and storing large quantities of hay a lot easier. Key to the rig was

Hay storage barns, such as this red-and-white example in Lee, Illinois, are used to store large quantities of feed. A mechanized elevator cuts down on the manpower required to stock the mow. ©2003 Howard Ande, Coolstock.com

the hayfork, a large metal claw that clamped onto the loose hay delivered by wagon. Some variations used a sling made of wooden slats and rope—a setup that was laid underneath the hay before it was loaded. Once the hay was delivered to the barn, the ropes were raised and attached to the hay carrier lifting rope. Then draft horses pulled on the rope to hoist the hay skyward and through the haymow door.

From here, the hay carrier moved along a metal (or wooden) track suspended from the ceiling. When the hay was in the right place, a worker released the latch and dropped the bundle by pulling the rope. Although it was still a labor-intensive chore, farmers packed the mow with grass, clover, and alfalfa with more efficiency than ever before.

In the Midwest, barns were built with a different sort of roof. Builders used a cleverly engineered construction called a gambrel. Named after the distinctive bent

Upon the advent of more efficient hay processing machinery, traditional hay bales were replaced by large round bales like those pictured here. ©2003 Howard Ande, Coolstock.com

The gambrel roof design was widely used by farmers who desired plenty of storage space. ©2003 Keith Baum, Coolstock.com

shape that defines the lower part of an animal's leg, the gambrel-style roof stood out among the single-pitch, bread-and-butter roof treatments indicative of Dutch, English, and Pennsylvania-German barns. Its chief characteristic was the combination of two different roof pitches symmetrical to each side of the ridgepole. At the roof peak, the angle was shallow. Halfway down to the pitch break, it became much steeper and continued this way down to the eaves.

In effect, this almost-vertical angle created both a roof and a wall. Inside, the tight triangle of space that was once wasted at each side of the mow was eliminated. A person could stand completely upright almost to the outer reaches of either side. The design provided more than enough "walk-around-without-bumping-your-head" space and allowed for storage of a super-sized portion of hay.

Besides its increased efficiency in terms of space, the gambrel configuration was also simpler and cheaper to build. It was constructed using a building process called balloon framing, which reduced the complexity of interior framework by substituting numerous 2-inch-thick planks. The structural loads once handled by a single massive timber were distributed among smaller pieces of wood joined together. More trusses were needed, but overall, the amount of wood used to construct the barn was decreased substantially.

As always happens when progress overtakes the status quo, the new assemblyline barn-building processes that saved the farmer time and money also eliminated the need for craftsmanship. Balloon frame structures didn't require painstaking joinery techniques. With minimal skill, carpenters could easily assemble the many identical and precut pieces of lumber to form wall frames and roof trusses. The process of joining timbers with wooden pegs also became an extinct art. Cheap, mass-produced nails were used to fasten the wood together. The generic barn roof had officially arrived.

Some design beauty did manage to survive, however. The striking Gothic roof, or rainbow roof as it is often called, stole the show as a space-conscious offshoot from the gambrel. The bow-truss design was promoted around 1915 by commercial mail-order firms that sold self-contained construction kits. The upper loft was expanded with a series of built-up rafters cut to a precise curve to create a smooth, continuous arch. Lauded for its ability to withstand the extreme winds of the open prairie, the Gothic roof gained a great amount of popularity in regions with extreme climates, such as North Dakota.

Due to their massive feed storage capabilities, both the gambrel- and Gothic-roof barns became a favored choice for the construction

This Steamboat Springs, Colorado, barn is a combination of chinked logs and clapboard. It has seen more than its share of hard winters and hot summers. ©2003 Sylvester Allred, Coolstock.com

While the barn in this Eldena, Illinois, scene is weathered by time and the elements, the accompanying grain storage silo with tile exterior looks as good as it did the day it was built. This is a graphic example of the material's staying power. ©2003 Howard Ande, Coolstock.com.

of dairy barns. Dairy farms grew in number during the second half of the nineteenth century. They popped up throughout the country and established an unofficial nexus in the Midwest. Cows in that region produced superior milk, and enterprising dairy farmers turned it into a variety of consumable products, including cream, butter, and cheese.

Because dairies were in constant use throughout the year, they demanded a significant amount of durability from their barn structures. A barn's size was determined by the milking capabilities of the farmer and was in direct relation to how much family or hired help there was on hand. The more cows that could be milked, the larger the barn needed to be in order to house them.

Other special considerations included the need for a fully weatherproofed enclosure so the interior climate could be regulated. Before there was electricity to power lights or fans, a row of windows on each of the eaves sides provided a prodigious amount of natural lighting and ventilation when necessary. Before milking machines were invented, cows were milked by hand, and the farmhands needed all the light they could get to execute their jobs.

Inside the dairy barn, accommodations were made to keep the cows happy, too. Dairy farmers know Holsteins and Guernseys are sensitive animals. Interior features took into account the preferences of these often-nervous creatures. Farmers balanced the ambient light, temperature, and outside distractions to maximize milk output. This wasn't always an easy job. For example,

The modern red barn with white trim is complete with haymow access, ventilation louvers, service entry, and shuttered windows. ©2003 Bruce Leighty, Coolstock.com

Without a defined ridge, the rainbow roof of this Utah barn has a distinctive appearance. The large, double doors in the haymow, with their unusual, angular track mounting, hint at the massive storage space inside. ©2003 Sylvester Allred, Coolstock.com

Lodge pole pine, cedar, and other coniferous woods were routinely used to build barns in the northern regions of the West. This barn in British Columbia also displays the hunting prowess of its owner. ©2003 Sylvester Allred, Coolstock.com

The Gothic influences of this Hope, Minnesota, brick barn are clearly evident. Here, a decoratively tiled silo is attached to the main structure via a smaller interpretation of the larger barn. ©2003 Bruce Leighty, Coolstock.com

Because dairy cows must be protected from the cold in the winter, dairy barns are built to more exacting standards. Inside, the cows enjoy an environment conducive to the production of milk. ©2003 Keith Baum, Coolstock.com

farmers replaced wood flooring with concrete because it was easier to keep clean. However, they then had to worry about how the cows would react to the cold floors in the winter and how the change might affect milk production. In this case, the farmers learned that using straw for bedding helped insulate the cold floor in the winter.

As the western, prairie, dairy, gambrel, and Gothic arch barns bolstered the diversity of farm architecture, an invention known as a silo added a new dimension to the family farm. According to historian Wayne D. Rasmussen, author of *Readings in the History of American Agriculture*, the first upright wooden silo was erected by Fred Hatch of McHenrey County, Illinois, in 1873. Farmers who cultivated the land and provided for cattle were quick to size up its benefit and readily adopted it as a standard part of operations.

The exterior siding of this saltbox-style barn in Kaneville, Illinois, is evidence of an architectural evolution. From the mismatched planks on the shed portion, one can surmise that this was a later addition. ©2003 Howard Ande, Coolstock.com

While a large majority of barns are painted red, there's something to be said for the weathered, silvered wood typical of the naturally aged barn. ©2003 Keith Baum, Coolstock.com

Peak projections, or beaks, provided a certain amount of protection from the elements when loading hay into the mow. This Steamboat Springs, Colorado, barn provided easy access with a strategically mounted ladder. ©2003 Sylvester Allred, Coolstock.com

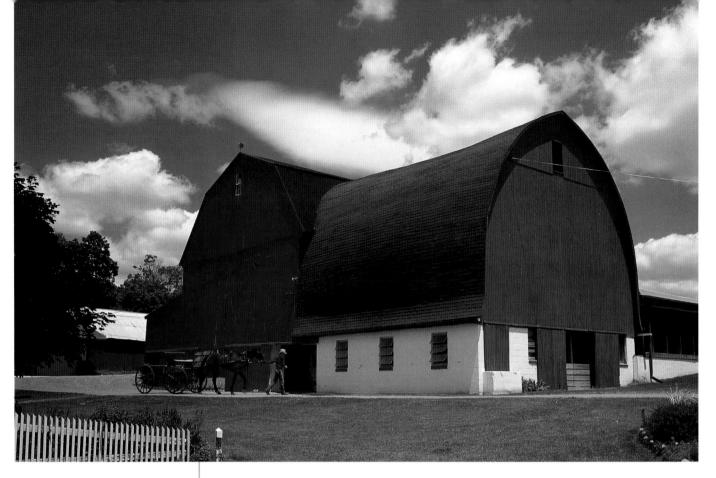

The Gothic and gambrel roof designs join forces to form a unique combination for this modern horse farm in Farmersville, Pennsylvania. ©2003 Keith Baum, Coolstock.com

The silo may seem simplistic to those unschooled in the science of agriculture, but the principles involved are quite scientific. It's more than just a bin to store fodder. It is a bona fide processing container that promotes preservation and maximizes nutrition. When silage breaks down, lactic acid (like the kind found in milk) and acetic acid (as in vinegar) are produced. This natural process creates a type of preservative effect that inhibits the spoilage of plant matter. This acid content also dictates just how nutritional the fodder will be and whether the animals will eat it.

Silos aren't restricted to just storing animal feed. Before these manmade towers came along, feed was often housed in a crib barn, a specialized structure used to store fodder and feed corn. Crib barns were built in many areas of the country but were seen more frequently in the South and Southeast. In the rural areas delineated by the present day borders of North Carolina, Virginia, Kentucky, Tennessee, Arkansas, and other regions throughout the Appalachian and Ozark mountains, crib barns were prominent structures where farming reigned.

Designed with simplicity in mind, the configuration of the basic crib barn was straightforward and harkened back to a time when rustic structures were still made from rough logs. The double crib barn was the standard prototype and was based

upon the arrangement of two storage areas, or cribs, spaced at a wagon's width distance from each other. Here, a central driveway ran between the two bins. Doors were installed in the front of each bin, adjacent to either side of the driveway to allow access.

Both of the compartments were made of logs, stacked in a horizontal manner, and left unchinked with air space between the timbers. Some variations of the corncrib were modified in regards to the internal division of the main cribs and doubled the storage arrangement to four separate compartments. Above, a cantilevered construction that looked much like an ordinary barn straddled the cribs and had an overhang at the front, back, and sides. Sometimes the cribs faced an extended, covered gallery that ran across the front and was supported by posts planted in the ground. This raised structural box was finished with vertical clapboard and topped with a conventional pitched roof covered with wood shingles. A distinctive cutout in the shape of a partial octagon punctuated the center of each wall and created the drive-through clearance farmers needed to pull their wagons through. The crib barn worked exactly the way it was expected to work, and perhaps that was the idea behind

Near Mt. Joy, Pennsylvania, the Hoffman Farm barn uses a tiled silo for housing fodder. It is conveniently attached to the base of the barn, making it easy to feed the livestock inside. *©2003 Keith Baum, Coolstock.com*

Located near Sleeping Bear Dunes, Michigan, this unabashed Gothic barn is unique in its artful treatment of storage silos (with dormer windows) and rooftop cupolas.

many of the American barns that emerged from the westward movement. Wherever crops were grown and animals were raised, newly designed structures followed the exact dictates of those who constructed them. From the mid-1800s to the dawn of the nineteenth century, the specialization and growth of the farmer created a change in barn styling and architecture. The barn was made over to suit new purposes and galloped boldly forth to become a true American creation and the pride of the prairies.

The gambrel roof was a boon to farmers when it was first introduced. With the added space, enough food could be stored to feed the animals through the winter months. ©2003 Keith Baum, Coolstock.com

When farming first began in the North American colonies, the production of grain was at the forefront. Today operations like this Archbold, Ohio, farm concentrate on raising livestock, an endeavor augmented by the capabilities of the modern silo. ©2003 Keith Baum, Coolstock.com

When commercially manufactured metal ventilators first came on the market, they were enthusiastically adopted by barn builders. They saved construction time and enhanced airflow with their optimized designs.
©2003 Keith Baum, Coolstock.com

Chapter Six

Eclectic Barn

A Building of Diversity

Why are barns painted red? According to historical accounts, the practice of coloring barns a scarlet hue is centuries old. Some say the color was used because farmers had an abundant supply of stock blood at their disposal. To produce a cheap paint, they mixed it with milk. Others presume that this preference of tint was born of Scandinavian practices where farmers used it to imitate brick and thus imply wealth.

The most plausible explanation is that European farmers used linseed oil—a tawny-colored oil derived from the flax plant—to seal the bare wood on their barns. In reality, the color that resulted was more like a burnt orange, not the intense, saturated shade that we see today. The truth is that the color known as classic "barn red" didn't get its punch until painters added iron oxide and milk of lime (calcium hydroxide suspended in water) to the concoction.

Since iron oxide and limestone were cheap and plentiful, farmers found the liquefied combination of rust and rock dust to be a cost-effective alternative to expensive, commercially manufactured paints. As a pleasant side effect, the ferrous ingredient also inhibited the wood decay. Rust keeps the formation of fungus, molds, and moss in check, reduces the quantity of trapped moisture in the grain, and increases the overall life of wood siding.

The temperature and humidity inside this classic tobacco-curing barn may be adjusted at will by way of its hinged, vertical side panels.

©2003 Keith Baum, Coolstock.com

The leaves of freshly harvested tobacco are hung in an inverted configuration and await curing in this Martindale, Pennsylvania, tobacco barn. ©2003 Keith Baum, Coolstock.com

Iron oxide's preservative quality was welcome news to the New England farmer since the barn, its accompanying outbuildings, and the living quarters required a considerable amount of exterior siding. Protecting all of this square footage with paint was a costly and labor-intensive process. Replacing warped or rotted boards also took valuable time away from other, more important duties.

Not all farm structures were defined by four exterior walls. In New England and parts of Canada, farmers who lived and worked in a connected barn had a few less square feet of exterior siding to worry about. The practical format got its start during the nineteenth century when farmers began to diversify operations in the face of a competitive market. At the time, all kinds of home industries sprang up, requiring a diverse range of shed, shacks, and workrooms to store tools and materials.

As farmers began to add onto existing barns and farmhouses, it was obvious that connecting two closely positioned structures would save time and materials. In the best-case scenario, the house was in close proximity to the barn. In this situation, storage rooms could be built in between the two and eliminate the need for two extra walls.

A number of distinct arrangements appeared to characterize the connected barn, or compound approach. The first was the inline format, an arrangement that aligned the farmhouse, storage room, and barn along the gable ends in one single

A combination of iron oxide and milk of lime created the red paint that coated so many barns. That stereotypical barn "look" can be spotted in all 50 states and Canada. ©Bruce Leighty, Coolstock.com

North Plato, Illinois, has its share of gambrel-roof barns. The town is also home to a tapestry of related styles that form the colorful pastiche of American barns. ©2003 Howard Ande, Coolstock.com

row. In many cases, the kitchen provided the point of access to the intermediary structure and allowed quick and practical access to the barn. On a cold and rainy day, farmers didn't have to worry about bundling up, putting their boots on, and braving the wind to feed the stock. They simply opened a door in the kitchen, walked through an adjoining woodshed, and entered the barn at the other end.

Another popular configuration was the "ell," a connected layout defined by two structures attached at the gable ends and joined with a third building on the eaves side that was set at 90 degrees in relation to the other structures. Variations of this grouping included the U-shaped, or square, compound, an arrangement that created a convenient, sheltered enclave. This courtyard could be used for outdoor activities or as a pen for animals.

In spite of its practical convenience, the connected barn had one major drawback. When one of the structures caught fire, the rest of the buildings were sure to burn down along with it. Stone firewalls addressed the flaw, but they were only practical when new construction allowed their installation and integration into the plan. When combined with higher insurance costs, the fire risk associated with the connected barn dampened its widespread use.

While connected barns satisfied the demands of many farm industries, they were inadequate when it came to curing and processing tobacco. Because of the combustive qualities of the drying leaves, the risk of fire was a big deterrent to using the compound approach. In addition, barns that were specially constructed to store

Meramec Caverns was a Missouri roadside attraction located on old Route 66. It could also be seen in painted advertisements on the side of barns. ©2003 Bruce Leighty, Coolstock.com

and dry tobacco crops had to be much larger and longer than other barns. This increased size made it impractical to position a tobacco barn near a farmhouse or other building since access roads and cross-traffic would be hindered. The high volume of crops that rotated in and out of the barn called for a different sort of convenience. A tobacco barn relied on a setup that could facilitate the quick transport of the harvested crop from field to barn. In this case, an independent structure close to the fields was more practical.

Tobacco was an important cash crop for the colonies and became a viable commercial enterprise during the early 1600s. Shortly after Virginian John Rolfe discovered that a certain variety of tobacco imported from the West Indies thrived in the local soil, the industry took off. Until the Revolutionary War, most of the smoking and chewing tobacco and snuff was exported to England, but after 1776, manufacturers produced it for domestic use. By the 1830s, the nation's growing addiction to smoking products made tobacco farming a lucrative endeavor.

As expected, the growing interest in tobacco farming stirred new directions in barn architecture. Tobacco growers needed a dedicated, stand-alone structure that was used primarily for drying the sap from newly harvested leaves. It also had to be large enough to hang the cut plants without crowding them, leave ample room for workers to move around, and be large enough to allow the air to circulate.

Growing corn is still a viable occupation for many American farmers. The three-bay, eaves-entry, English barn also remains a viable configuration for barn architecture. ©2003 Howard Ande, Coolstock.com

With the aid of a horse-drawn cart, an Amish man and his sons harvest tobacco by hand near Weavertown, Pennsylvania. ©2003 Keith Baum, Coolstock.com

The resulting prototype featured vertical ventilation slats positioned along both sides of the barn, a type of exterior siding that was unique to the tobacco barn. Air curing, a slow process that produces chemical changes in tobacco to enhance its flavor and aroma, was enabled by opening and closing the hinged louvers to control the temperature and humidity.

Of course, the idea of a tailor-made building constructed to satisfy regional expectations and a diversity of crops resonated far beyond the tobacco fields of the Connecticut River Valley and North Carolina. By the dawn of the twentieth century, a myriad of barn variations appeared in all regions of the country. Whether they were hop-drying barns in the Northwest, dairy barns in the Midwest, or rice barns in the Carolinas, the buildings all shared a common denominator: practicality. During the time when feeding the nation was the exclusive domain of the American farm, there wasn't a barn built that didn't have a specific job or purpose.

During the 1910s and 1920s, the ongoing demand for practical barns sustained a number of mail-order barn suppliers, including the Gordon-Van Tine Company of Davenport, Iowa, and the venerable Chicago catalog giant Sears, Roebuck, and

Many tobacco barns incorporate hinged side panels on their exteriors. When curing operations are underway, the vertical openings are visual evidence that another crop is undergoing the slow process of air curing. ©2003 Keith Baum, Coolstock.com.

Company. The do-it-yourself assembly barns were sold as complete kits and could be customized by incrementally adding to the length and width of the structure. The railroads delivered them to the nearest train depot where horse-drawn wagons hauled the pieces the rest of the way to the building site.

Sears sold a variety of affordable barns, and the models ranged from complicated to conservative. For instance, a gambrel-roof structure that measured 30 by 54 feet was touted to stable 12 milk cows and 6 horses. The asking price was an affordable $480. Best of all, there were no hidden charges in this 1911 catalog offering. Sears included all of the yellow pine lumber required for the framing and flooring. The kit also included the shingles, door and window hardware, and sash. Customers also had the privilege of choosing the color of the paint and were supplied with just enough of it to be able to apply two coats to the exterior.

Barns with names like "Prairie Chief," "Springfield," or "Cyclone" could be ordered by simply sending in an order with a bank check. A short while later, the barn arrived—premeasured, precut, and ready to put together. A little hard work and a few hundred hours later, the farmer had a finished barn and a sense of accomplishment.

Nevertheless, nothing that came from a kit could equal the quintessential homespun qualities of the log barn. Based on a form of construction brought over to North America by the Swedes who settled in the Delaware Valley in 1638 and by the

A prodigious use of windows provides natural light to the interior of this side-entry, English-style barn, near Two Creeks, Wisconsin. ©2003 Howard Ande, Coolstock.com

A variety of barns, outbuildings, silos, and ancillary structures comprise this farm south of Strasburg, Pennsylvania. ©2003 Keith Baum, Coolstock.com

115

Chinked log barn construction has been used in many areas, including the Appalachian regions, Texas, and Montana. ©2003 Sylvester Allred, Coolstock.com

Germans in 1710, the log style is regarded by many as perhaps the earliest method used to build shelters and dwellings.

Log structures—buildings that were made of horizontally laid timbers notched at the corners—once dominated the eastern half of Texas. During the height of the structure's popularity, the "single-pen" house was the most common log building. This simple structure was Spartan at best and consisted of a single, 16-foot square room attached to a rear shed. Side gables and an exterior chimney pulled the floor plan together. A variation of this design was the double-pen, a floor plan characterized by two full-sized rooms or pens. These compartments were separated by an open breezeway without doors and, in the colloquialism of the region, were referred to by the people of East Texas as dog-runs.

Barns constructed entirely of logs evolved along the same track and borrowed from these design and layout variations to suit individual use and needs. With their representative saddle-notched corners, hand-hewn log barns managed to migrate

Tobacco curing in the barn and corn growing in the field illustrate the industrious nature of the Pennsylvania Amish. ©2003 Keith Baum, Coolstock.com

even farther west than Texas and cropped up in the lodge pole, pine-rich regions of Colorado, Montana, and Wyoming. Further to the east, the Appalachian areas of the country also saw extensive use of log construction for farmhouses and barns.

Harley Warrick would have gladly told you how log barns affected his business. He spent 55 years traveling the highways and byways of Appalachia and the Midwest and stopped here and there to paint colorful Mail Pouch Tobacco billboards on the side of roadside barns. He began his sign-painting career in 1945 when he was fresh out of the Army. At age 21, he was offered his first (and subsequently his last) job when he crossed paths with a team of Mail Pouch painters who happened to be repainting an ad on his parents' dairy barn in Belmont, Ohio.

This structure includes horizontal slat siding with air space, a gambrel roof, double doors, and a red paint job. This is the classic example of the American barn. ©2003 Bruce Leighty, Coolstock.com

"Chew Mail Pouch Tobacco. Treat Yourself to the Best," became Warrick's creed. It was a slogan he painted on roughly 4,000 barns during the long run of his career. Amazingly, he painted all of them without templates and instead relied on his eye for detail and proportion. He sometimes completed as many as a dozen signs in one week.

Prospective barns were hand-picked according to their usability. If it had windows that might interfere with the lettering, the barn wasn't a good candidate. A broad area of wood was the best bet, especially if it faced the highway and could be seen without the motorist taking his or her eyes off the road. It was a win-win deal all the way around: farmers got a new paint job on their barns, and the Bloch Brothers Tobacco Company of Wheeling, West Virginia, got a visible venue for their advertising message. In some cases, magazine subscriptions, supplies of tobacco, or a modest leasing fee helped sweeten the deal.

After Lady Bird Johnson's Highway Beautification Act roared through Congress in 1966, gaudy billboards located near federal highways were doomed. An exception was made for the Mail Pouch signs, which were exempted from the laws in 1974. Even so, the Mail Pouch company unofficially phased out the barn ads after the 1960s. It did, however, keep Warrick on the company payroll to keep the existing signs fresh. At one time, as many as 10,000 ads graced the sides of barns from Florida to Washington state.

Mail Pouch Tobacco is perhaps the most recognized product advertised on barn billboards. While advertising on barns was banned during the 1960s, interest has since rekindled. Today there is a certain cachet to owning a barn emblazoned with the slogan, "Treat yourself to the best." ©2003 Keith Baum, Coolstock.com

Today, further endangered by a total ban on tobacco advertisements, only a handful of survivors remain. The era of the whimsically painted barn along the roadside has come to a close.

In some ways, the era of the classic American barn has come to a close as well. Whether we like it or not, another part of our cultural heritage is slipping away. Its reason for being is superceded by factory farming operations and global conglomerates that answer only to the stockholders' quest for profits. These days, America's rich heritage of English, Dutch, Pennsylvania-German, and a multitude of other barn styles is in decay—the structures forlorn, neglected, or abandoned from disuse. Some are now obsolete for modern farming, while others are deemed too expensive to maintain as family heirlooms.

Fortunately, there is some hope. In 1987, the National Trust for Historic Preservation and *Successful Farming* magazine launched Barn Again!, an organization

As we head into the future, barns are being built from prefabricated plans, and kits have transformed the age-old craft of barn building into a do-it-yourself project for the weekends. ©*2003 Dan Harlow, Coolstock.com*

119

Log barns were most often seen in the far Western states where pest-resistant woods, such as lodge pole pine, were plentiful. This gambrel-roof model, complete with an added shed, was spied in Northern Colorado. ©2003 Sylvester Allred, Coolstock.com

With its rooftop cupola shuttered for the winter and silo piled high with fodder, this Colts Neck, New Jersey, farm stands ready for winter. ©2003 Ron Saari, Coolstock.com

The open doors of this tobacco barn near Martindale, Pennsylvania, reveal a bicycle and horse-drawn buggy, common modes of transportation used by the Plain sect Mennonites. ©2003 Keith Baum, Coolstock.com

dedicated to secure our nation's agricultural architecture and preserve it for future generations. By means of an Internet website, telephone technical assistance hotline, educational workshops, rehabilitation guides, exhibits, and other informative events, it provides information to help owners of historic barns rehabilitate them and put them back to productive use on farms and ranches.

One barn at a time, Barn Again! has disproved the widely accepted premise that new is better. The program has changed the attitudes of many people unaware of the American barn's plight and has shown how historic barns can be adapted for new farming uses ranging from dairy, hog, and cattle operations to machinery and grain storage. Time and time again, Barn Again! has demonstrated how preservation techniques can be a cost-effective alternative to razing an old barn and putting up a brand new building. To drive the point home, the organization presents a yearly award for the best examples of historic barns rehabilitated for farming.

Hay rake disks stand ready for use outside this hay storage barn in Ephrata, Pennsylvania. ©2003 Keith Baum, Coolstock.com

Barn Again! is an important charter because barns represent a time when individuals made it on their own without government intervention. Surviving barns, in all of their eclectic forms, are living reminders of how our nation's first settlers carved out a living from the land and pressed natural resources into service. They recall a time when craftsmanship and quality took precedence, and life was guided by the golden rule. They break through the noise of the twenty-first century with a reserved confidence and a renewed purpose. The American barn is as a bona fide icon of liberty and freedom, no matter what the style or structure.

The connected barn concept of this Michigan setup has a protected byre, or courtyard, at the center. A single row of fencing is all that's needed to keep the animals in. ©2003 Keith Baum, Coolstock.com

The large dinner bell mounted atop the adjoining outbuilding of this Holmdel, New Jersey, connected barn complex suggests a farming operation that supported quite a number of farmhands. ©2003 Ron Saari, Coolstock.com

The owner of this Franklin, Indiana, farm shows his sense of humor with a ring of electrically operated traffic signals placed around the top of his silo. ©2003 Bruce Leighty, Coolstock.com

The owners of this farm in Bernsville, Pennsylvania, have gone all out to show their Christmas cheer. It wasn't until the Rural Electrification Act of 1936 was signed into law by President Franklin D. Roosevelt that the first big push to bring electricity to America's rural areas began to make scenes like this one possible. ©2003 Keith Baum, Coolstock.com

The flared treatment of its gambrel roof gives this Evart, Michigan, a distinctively light feeling. ©2003 Keith Baum, Coolstock.com

This gambrel-roofed beauty has been converted into an antique shop. It still exudes a marked sense of sturdiness and an ability to get the job done—even if that is selling knickknacks to bargain hunters and tourists. ©2003 Keith Baum, Coolstock.com

Index